California
Legal Research

CAROLINA ACADEMIC PRESS
LEGAL RESEARCH SERIES

Tenielle Fordyce-Ruff, Series Editor
Suzanne E. Rowe, Series Editor Emerita

❧

Arizona, Third Edition — Tamara S. Herrera

Arkansas, Second Edition — Coleen M. Barger, Cheryl L. Reinhart &
Cathy L. Underwood

California, Fourth Edition — Aimee Dudovitz, Sarah Laubach & Suzanne E. Rowe

Colorado, Second Edition — Robert Michael Linz

Connecticut — Jessica G. Hynes

Federal, Second Edition — Mary Garvey Algero, Spencer L. Simons,
Suzanne E. Rowe, Scott Childs & Sarah E. Ricks

Florida, Fourth Edition — Barbara J. Busharis, Jennifer LaVia & Suzanne E. Rowe

Georgia — Nancy P. Johnson, Elizabeth G. Adelman & Nancy J. Adams

Idaho, Third Edition — Tenielle Fordyce-Ruff

Illinois, Second Edition — Mark E. Wojcik

Iowa, Second Edition — John D. Edwards, Karen L. Wallace & Melissa H. Weresh

Kansas — Joseph A. Custer & Christopher L. Steadham

Kentucky, Second Edition — William A. Hilyerd, Kurt X. Metzmeier & David J. Ensign

Louisiana, Third Edition — Mary Garvey Algero

Massachusetts, Second Edition — E. Joan Blum & Shaun B. Spencer

Michigan, Third Edition — Cristina D. Lockwood & Pamela Lysaght

Minnesota — Suzanne Thorpe

Mississippi — Kristy L. Gilliland

Missouri, Third Edition — Wanda M. Temm & Julie M. Cheslik

New York, Third Edition — Elizabeth G. Adelman, Theodora Belniak,
Courtney L. Selby & Brian Detweiler

North Carolina, Third Edition — Brenda D. Gibson, Julie L. Kimbrough,
Laura P. Graham & Nichelle J. Perry

North Dakota — Anne E. Mullins & Tammy R. Pettinato

Ohio, Second Edition — Sara Sampson, Katherine L. Hall & Carolyn Broering-Jacobs

Oklahoma — Darin K. Fox, Darla W. Jackson & Courtney L. Selby

Oregon, Fourth Edition, Revised Printing — Suzanne E. Rowe & Megan Austin

Pennsylvania, Second Edition — Barbara J. Busharis, Catherine M. Dunn,
Bonny L. Tavares & Carla P. Wale

Tennessee, Second Edition — Scott Childs, Sibyl Marshall & Carol McCrehan Parker

Texas, Second Edition — Spencer L. Simons

Washington, Second Edition — Julie Heintz-Cho, Tom Cobb & Mary A. Hotchkiss

West Virginia, Second Edition — Hollee Schwartz Temple

Wisconsin — Patricia Cervenka & Leslie Behroozi

Wyoming, Second Edition — Debora A. Person & Tawnya K. Plumb

❧

California
Legal Research

Fourth Edition

Aimee Dudovitz
Sarah Laubach
Suzanne E. Rowe

Tenielle Fordyce-Ruff, Series Editor
Suzanne E. Rowe, Series Editor Emerita

Carolina Academic Press
Durham, North Carolina

Library of Congress Cataloging-in-Publication Data

Names: Dudovitz, Aimee, author. | Laubach, Sarah, author. | Rowe,
    Suzanne E., 1961- author.
Title: California legal research / by Aimee Dudovitz, Sarah Laubach,
    Suzanne E. Rowe.
Description: Fourth edition. | Durham, North Carolina : Carolina
    Academic Press, LLC, [2019] | Series: Legal research series | Includes
    bibliographical references and index.
Identifiers: LCCN 2019021488 | ISBN 9781531015619 (alk. paper)
Subjects: LCSH: Legal research--California.
Classification: LCC KFC74 .D83 2019 | DDC 340.072/0794--dc23
LC record available at https://lccn.loc.gov/2019021488

e-ISBN 978-1-5310-1562-6

CAROLINA ACADEMIC PRESS

700 Kent Street
Durham, North Carolina 27701
Telephone (919) 489-7486
Fax (919) 493-5668
www.cap-press.com

Printed in the United States of America.

Dedicated

to Joshua and Jeffrey
A.D.

to Ilan
S.L.

and to Didi and Hether
S.E.R.

Summary of Contents

Contents

List of Tables, Figures, and Appendices

Tables

Figures

Appendices

Series Note

The Legal Research Series published by Carolina Academic Press includes titles from many states around the country as well as a separate text on federal legal research. The goal of each book is to provide law students, practitioners, paralegals, college students, laypeople, and librarians with the essential elements of legal research in each jurisdiction. Unlike more bibliographic texts, the Legal Research Series books seek to explain concisely both the sources of legal research and the process for conducting legal research effectively.

Preface and Acknowledgments for the Fourth Edition

This fourth edition of *California Legal Research* continues the goal of prior editions: to explain clearly, but concisely, the sources and the process for researching California law. While much has changed in the three years since the third edition was published, we prioritized essential updates and tighter explanations to keep this edition familiar to readers of the prior editions. This edition increasingly emphasizes online research, while including guidance with print sources that remain relevant. The chapter on researching judicial opinions, for instance, has been substantially revised to embrace the shift to online case research.

As in prior editions, we emphasize Lexis and Westlaw products because they are the most widely used and the most relevant to California-specific research, and we attempt to present balanced coverage of Lexis and Westlaw. To make the book more readable, we have in the text used the abbreviated term "Westlaw" to refer to Westlaw Edge and omitted the registered trademark symbol above that term as well as "Lexis," "Lexis Advance," and "Shepard's." We are grateful to the publishers for permission to include small portions of their books and online products in this text. This edition reduces its coverage of Bloomberg Law, which is most useful in researching business law topics and dockets, rather than general research.

In this fourth edition, we express our deep appreciation to Hether Macfarlane. She was the lead author of the first two editions, and she continued as an author of the third edition. Her work is still reflected throughout this new edition, particularly the chapters on judicial opinions, statutes, and constitutions. Those chapters and the one on researching judicial opinions were updated by our new co-author Sarah Laubach, who brought new insights to the entire project. Aimee Dudovitz was responsible for updating the chapters on legislative history, administrative law, and secondary sources. Professor Dudovitz continues as our lead author, unifying the voices of three authors and coordinating the production process. Suzanne Rowe updated the chapters on the research process, research techniques, citators, research strategies, and citation. Portions of this book are based on *Oregon Legal Research*[1] and are used with permission. The final product was again a collaborative effort.

Aimee Dudovitz
Sarah Laubach
Suzanne E. Rowe

---

1. Particularly, the opening of Chapter 1, the guidance on reading cases in Chapter 3, general discussions of secondary sources in Chapter 10, and the explanation of case citations in Chapter 12 draw from that book, as do other books in the Legal Research Series.

California
Legal Research

Chapter 1

The Research Process and Legal Analysis

I. Legal Research and Legal Analysis

Researching California's laws is essential to solving legal problems. Attorneys conduct research when representing litigants in court, recommending new statutes to the legislature, advising businesses, or otherwise assisting clients. The process of finding California law on a particular issue can be straightforward. Most attorneys search online using words likely to appear in the text of relevant legal documents. Working with print sources, attorneys often begin with an index, find references to entries that appear relevant, and read those sections of the book. Whether working online or in print, attorneys ensure that the documents are the most recent statement of the law.

What makes legal research challenging is that legal analysis is required throughout the process. Choosing search terms, knowing whether a document is relevant, and ensuring that the document is current all require legal analysis. To ensure you conduct thorough and effective legal research, this book supplements its focus on legal research with the fundamentals of legal analysis.

II. Types of Legal Authority

The documents that comprise California law are the state's constitution, statutes, administrative and court rules, and judicial opinions. The goal of legal research is to find those documents that control a client's situation. In other words, you are searching for primary, mandatory authority.

Primary authority is law produced by government bodies with law-making power. Legislatures write statutes, courts write judicial opinions, and administrative agencies write regulations. *Secondary authority* includes all other legal sources, such as treatises, law review articles, legal encyclopedias, and blogs.

Table 1-1. Examples of Authority in California Research

	Mandatory Authority	Persuasive Authority
Primary Authority	California statutes California Supreme Court cases California regulations	Washington statutes Oregon Supreme Court cases Nevada regulations
Secondary Authority	—	Law review articles Legal encyclopedias Treatises Restatements

They may be written by attorneys, judges, and law professors; by the editorial staff of publishing companies; or by law students. These secondary sources are designed to aid researchers in understanding the law and locating primary authority.

Primary authority from the controlling jurisdiction is called *mandatory authority*—authority that is binding on the court that would decide a conflict if it resulted in litigation. In a question of California law, mandatory authority includes California's constitution, statutes enacted by the California Legislature, California regulations, and opinions of the Supreme Court of California.[1] In contrast, *persuasive authority* is not binding, but courts may choose to follow it when it is relevant and well reasoned. Authority is merely persuasive if it is primary authority from a different jurisdiction or if it is not produced by a law-making body (i.e., secondary sources). In California legal research, examples of persuasive authority include a similar Washington statute, an opinion of an Oregon state court, and a law review article. As shown in Table 1-1, persuasive authority may be either primary or secondary authority, while mandatory authority is always primary.

In California, as in each state, the state's constitution is the highest legal authority. Statutes come next in the legal hierarchy, followed by administrative regulations, and then judicial opinions that interpret statutes and regulations.

---

1. An opinion from the California Court of Appeal is binding on trial courts throughout California if the California Supreme Court has not addressed a particular topic. *Auto Equity Sales, Inc. v. Superior Court of Santa Clara Cty.*, 57 Cal. 2d 450, 455–56 (1962). If the decisions of various California appellate districts conflict, the trial courts are free to choose among the conflicting decisions. *Id.* at 456.

However, a judicial opinion may hold that a statute violates the constitution or that a regulation is void because it exceeds an agency's powers. In California, a court can also "reform" or rewrite a state statute to avoid invalidating it on specific constitutional grounds when the intention of the legislature or the electorate is clear.[2] When no constitutional provision, statute, or administrative regulation is *on point* (i.e., relevant), the issue will be controlled by *common law*, also called judge-made law.[3]

III. Overview of the Research Process

Conducting effective legal research means following a process. This process leads to the authority that controls a legal issue as well as to commentary that may help you analyze new and complex legal matters. The outline in Table 1-2 presents the fundamental research process.

A. Prepare to Research

Before beginning to research, collect the available information about the project. Gather facts from client interviews, colleagues, documents in the client file, and other sources. At the same time, gather practical facts about your project, including the deadline and the research sources at your disposal. Also identify the legal issue you need to research. When you are working for a supervisor, that person might tell you what the issue is. If not, your first research might be aimed at determining the key legal issue to address. Next, be sure that you know the relevant jurisdiction. Your project might be governed by international law, federal law, state law, local law, or tribal law, or by a combination of those. This book assumes that California is the relevant jurisdiction.

Your last preparatory step is generating research terms. Legal research— whether online or in print—often begins with a list of words that are relevant to the topic of the research project. Even if you expect to enter a question into an online search engine, generating a thorough and thoughtful list of search terms is crucial to a successful search. Especially when researching an unfamiliar area of law, you will need a comprehensive list of words, terms, and phrases to lead you to law on point. These may be legal terms or common words that describe the client's situation.

---

2. *Kopp v. Fair Political Practices Comm'n*, 11 Cal. 4th 607, 615 (1995).

3. Common law is derived from judicial decisions, rather than statutes or constitutions. *Black's Law Dictionary* 334 (Bryan A. Garner ed., 10th ed., West 2014).

Table 1-2. Overview of the Research Process

1. **Prepare**
   Gather facts, identify the research issue, determine the relevant jurisdiction, and list research terms.

2. **Learn**
   Consult secondary sources, including treatises, legal encyclopedias, practice aids, and law review articles. These will provide context and background on your issue and might point to primary authority.

3. **Search**
   Look for enacted law in the relevant jurisdiction, including constitutional provisions, statutes, and administrative regulations. Gather citations to relevant cases.

4. **Read**
   Take time throughout your research to read carefully the authorities you are locating.

5. **Update**
   Use citators to update your legal authorities to ensure they are current and to find additional, relevant authorities.

6. **Finish**
   In general, your research is complete when there are no holes remaining in your analysis and when searches in different sources produce the same set of authorities.

To compile a comprehensive list of research terms, some researchers ask the journalistic questions: Who? What? How? Why? When? Where? Some researchers rely on sophisticated online algorithms to suggest additional terms. Whatever approach you prefer, generate a broad range of research terms regarding the facts, issues, and desired solutions of your client's situation. Include in the list both specific and general words. List synonyms and antonyms for each term, especially when working with print sources or less sophisticated online search engines. Using a legal dictionary or thesaurus—often provided by online services—may help to generate additional terms.

As an example of this first step in the research process, assume a client has suffered nightmares and anxiety attacks after the following scene at a restaurant in San Diego. He and his wife were having lunch at an outside table near the street. The man went inside to the restroom, and as he returned to the table he heard a car crash. He saw a table umbrella fall and felt pieces of glass from a shattered mirror. A car had jumped the curb and hit his wife. Although she eventually recovered from her serious injuries, he has continued to suffer serious emotional symptoms. Your supervisor asks you to research whether

Table 1-3. Generating Research Terms:
Journalistic Approach

Who:	Driver, spouse, husband, bystander
What:	Car accident, lingering symptoms, anxiety, nightmares
How:	Being near accident that injured spouse
Why:	Reckless driving, witnessing accident
When:	Daytime, lunch hour
Where:	Restaurant, San Diego, street side, near sidewalk

the client has a claim for negligent infliction of emotion distress against the driver, even though the client was merely an observer or bystander to the accident. You know that California is the relevant jurisdiction. Table 1-3 provides examples of research terms you might use to begin work on this project.

B. Learn About the Topic

Most lawyers begin researching an unfamiliar area of law by turning to secondary sources. These sources include books written by practicing attorneys, law review articles, and encyclopedia entries. They also include websites and blogs. Secondary sources are helpful because they summarize, explain, and sometimes analyze the law. Often a secondary source will be easier to understand initially than a constitutional provision, statute, regulation, or judicial opinion. Secondary sources are also helpful because they contain references to relevant primary authorities.

C. Search for Primary Authority

1. Finding Constitutional Provisions and Statutes

California's constitution is the highest legal authority on state matters. It begins with fundamental rights that are similar to those ensured by the federal constitution. Article I of the California Constitution provides, "All people are by nature free and independent and have inalienable rights. Among these are enjoying and defending life and liberty, acquiring, possessing, and protecting property, and pursuing and obtaining safety, happiness, and privacy." But the state constitution is not identical to the federal constitution, and it contains provisions that are more statutory in nature. For example, Article 10B of the California Constitution is known as the Marine Resources Protection Act of 1990; it prohibits the use of gill nets and trammel nets in certain zones.

The California Legislature has enacted statutes on many topics. Statutes are organized by subject matter in twenty-nine codes ranging from "Civil Procedure" to "Labor" to "Revenue and Taxation." A list of the twenty-nine codes is provided in Chapter 6 at Table 6-1. An example of a single statute is section 451 of the Penal Code, which sets the penalties for arson. See Figure 6-1.

2. Researching Administrative Law

California has over 200 state regulatory agencies. These agencies issue regulations on matters ranging from drivers' licenses to environmental protection. The regulations are codified in twenty-eight titles in the California Code of Regulations; these are listed in Table 8-2 in Chapter 8. An example of a regulation is provided in Figure 8-1. Agencies also decide disputes regarding the agencies' regulations.

3. Researching Judicial Opinions

Courts write judicial opinions to explain their decisions in the cases that come before them. Some opinions are based on statutory law; the courts in these cases apply the statutory requirements to the facts of the parties before them. Other opinions are based on administrative law; most often, these cases are appeals from decisions by administrative agencies. When no statute or administrative regulation controls, judicial opinions are based on the common law.

Judicial opinions are published in chronological order in books called *reporters*. There are multiple reporters for California opinions, which are covered in Chapter 3. Even when you read cases online, their citations are typically to print reporters. Appendices to Chapter 3 show the first screen of the same case as seen on Westlaw and Lexis, two premier sources for online legal research.

D. Read Authorities Carefully

One of the most important and time-consuming aspects of legal research is reading the authorities that you locate. While online services are making it increasingly easy to read, highlight, and save documents on their websites, do not underestimate the value of printing key authorities and reading them repeatedly in hard copy.

E. Update with Citators

After finding statutes, cases, and other authorities that address a research topic, you must ensure that these authorities represent the current law. This step is performed using *citators*. The process of using citators to ensure that authorities are still respected is called "updating." For example, a citator produces a list of authorities that have mentioned a case you have decided is relevant, along with indications of whether the authorities agreed with the case or not. Several samples of citator lists appear in Chapter 9. By reviewing these lists, you can learn whether that case has been reversed, overruled, distinguished, or followed.

Because citators provide lists of authorities, they are also effective finding tools. Entering the citation for one relevant case can quickly produce a list of other cases that may be relevant because they relied on a case you know is relevant.

F. Finish the Research

The goal of research is to solve a client's problem. If you immediately find a primary authority that answers the client's question, your research may be complete. Most research projects, however, do not have a clear answer. You will have to collect bits and pieces of information in various primary authorities to construct a solution that meets your client's goals. When there is no clear answer, it can be difficult to know when to stop researching. There are two checkpoints for knowing that research is nearing an end.

First, make an outline of your answer to the client's problems. When there are no analytical holes in the outline, you are likely finished researching. Second, in reviewing secondary sources, statutes, administrative law, and judicial opinions, and then updating relevant authorities, it is likely that you will begin to see the same authorities appear repeatedly. No longer finding new authorities is an excellent sign that your research has been thorough and you should stop looking for additional authorities.

G. Modify the Process

The fundamental research process should be customized for each research project. Consider whether you need to follow all six steps and whether to modify the order. If you are unfamiliar with an area of law, you should follow each step of the process in the order indicated in Table 1-2. Beginning with secondary sources will provide both context for the issues you must research and citations to relevant primary authority. As you gain experience in researching legal questions, you may choose to modify the process. For example, when you know that a situation is controlled by a statute, you may choose to begin with Step 3. Or when you know of a case that is on point, you may decide to read and update it immediately to find additional cases on the same point. Research strategies are discussed in more detail in Chapter 11.

IV. Researching the Law — Organization of This Text

Chapter 2 of this book explains fundamental search techniques for legal research. Most of the remaining chapters explain in depth how to research different legal resources.[4] Chapter 3 covers the California court system and judicial opinions, while Chapter 4 explains strategies for finding judicial opinions. This book covers case research first because most legal research includes finding and reading cases, even when other primary authority is on point. Chapter 5 addresses the California Constitution. Chapter 6 describes researching statutes, and Chapter 7 discusses legislative history research. Chapter 8 addresses administrative law, including regulations, agency decisions, and attorney general opinions.

After this focus on primary authority, Chapter 9 explains how to update legal authority using citators like KeyCite on Westlaw and Shepard's on Lexis. Chapter 10 covers secondary sources, the frequent starting point for research in an unfamiliar area of law. The discussion of secondary sources is delayed to emphasize their subordinate position relative to primary authority. Chapter 11 discusses research strategies as well as how to organize your research. If you benefit from seeing the big picture first, you might skim that chapter now and refer to it as you read more detailed explanations in the intervening chapters.

Chapter 12 provides an overview of the conventions lawyers follow in citing legal authority in their documents. In addition to discussing California citations under the *California Style Manual*,[5] this chapter introduces the two national citation manuals, the *ALWD Guide to Legal Citation*[6] and *The Bluebook:*

---

4. Law students using this book in a research class will most likely cover the chapters in a different order, reflecting the research strategies needed to complement their other coursework.

5. Edward W. Jessen, *California Style Manual* (4th ed. 2000) ("*CSM*").

6. ALWD & Coleen Barger, *ALWD Guide to Legal Citation* (6th ed. 2017) ("*ALWD Guide*").

A Uniform System of Citation.[7] While most citations in this book conform to the *ALWD Guide* and the *Bluebook,* cases are cited to official California reporters, reflecting the common practice among California lawyers.

---

7. *The Bluebook: A Uniform System of Citation* (The Columbia Law Review et al. eds., 20th ed. 2015) ("*Bluebook*").

Chapter 2

Legal Research Techniques

Lawyers conduct research using commercial online products, free online sources, government and law library websites, and print materials. While each of these resources is slightly different, some research techniques are effective regardless of the resource used. This chapter introduces the basic techniques for researching in online and print legal resources. The chapter begins with techniques for research in online products, focusing on Westlaw and Lexis because they have the most expansive databases and the most robust search options. Other online services are then introduced, followed by a review of print research techniques. Later chapters build on these basics and offer more advanced techniques and strategies.

I. Online Research Techniques

Many online tools can be used to conduct efficient and cost-effective legal research. Table 2-1 lists web addresses for government websites containing California primary authority, and Table 2-2 lists addresses for other legal research providers, including both commercial and free sites. Table 2-2 also includes two "gateway" sites supported by universities, Cornell University Law School's Legal Information Institute and Washburn University School of Law's WashLaw. These sites link to a variety of online resources.

If the information you need is available for free (e.g., on a government or university site, or on Google Scholar), think carefully before using a costly commercial provider. Sometimes a commercial provider's extensive database or sophisticated search engine will make the cost worthwhile, but you should consider the costs and efficiencies involved in every search.

Because Westlaw and Lexis are the primary commercial sites on which lawyers rely, they are the focus of this section. Other commercial, fee-based sites — including Bloomberg Law, Casemaker, Fastcase, and VersusLaw — are addressed briefly in this section and at the end of this chapter.

Table 2-1. Selected Government Websites for California Primary Authority

Type of Authority	Web Address
California Constitution and California Statutes	leginfo.legislature.ca.gov/faces/codes.xhtml
California Regulations	oal.ca.gov (click on "California Code of Regulations")
California Appellate Opinions	courts.ca.gov/opinions.htm

A. Finding a Legal Source by Citation

When working online, retrieving a document is as simple as typing the citation into a designated box on the proper screen. Typing *California Penal Code 451* into Lexis leads to the state statute defining arson and setting the punishment. Note that online services typically use the print citation to identify some documents, particularly cases. In other words, to retrieve a case from Lexis, you will enter the volume and page of the print reporter, along with that reporter's abbreviation. Typing *62 Cal. 4th 360* would retrieve the 2015 case *People v. Goolsby*, where the California Supreme Court interprets the arson statute and applies it to a specific fact pattern. Many online providers list accepted citation formats, which vary from one online site to another.

Table 2-2. Legal Research Providers

Service/Provider	Web Address
Bloomberg Law	bloomberglaw.com
Casemaker	casemakerx.com
Fastcase	fastcase.com
FindLaw	findlaw.com
Google Scholar	scholar.google.com
Lexis Advance	advance.lexis.com
VersusLaw	versuslaw.com
Westlaw	westlaw.com
Gateway Sites	
Cornell University Law School's Legal Information Institute	law.cornell.edu
Washburn University School of Law's WashLaw	washlaw.edu

B. Table-of-Contents Searching

A table of contents lists the major segments of a document or set of documents. As examples, the California Penal Code has a table of contents that lists all of the statutes in numerical order, and a book's table of contents lists each chapter. An online table of contents will often list only major headings on the initial screen. Subheadings may be accessed by clicking a symbol next to one of the headings; the symbol might be a plus sign or a triangle. On some services, you can either click on the name of a major heading, or check a box and click "Search" to access the table of contents. The advantages of skimming an online table of contents are (1) seeing how various issues and topics are related in that area of law, and (2) finding relevant portions of the document or database.

For example, to determine whether an injury that occurred at work is covered by California's workers' compensation laws, open the table of contents for California statutes on Westlaw. It is available under the link for "State Materials": click on "California" and then "California Statutes and Court Rules." Click on the heading "Labor Code" to view the major divisions of that code, including "Division 4. Workers' Compensation and Insurance." Subsequent clicks lead to the division's parts, then chapters, and finally individual statutes. See Figures 2-1 and 2-2.

Figure 2-1. Table-of-Contents Searching on Westlaw Edge

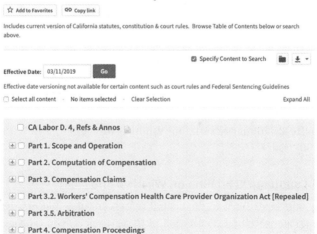

Source: Westlaw. Used with permission of Thomson Reuters.

Figure 2-2. Table-of-Contents Searching on California Legislative Site

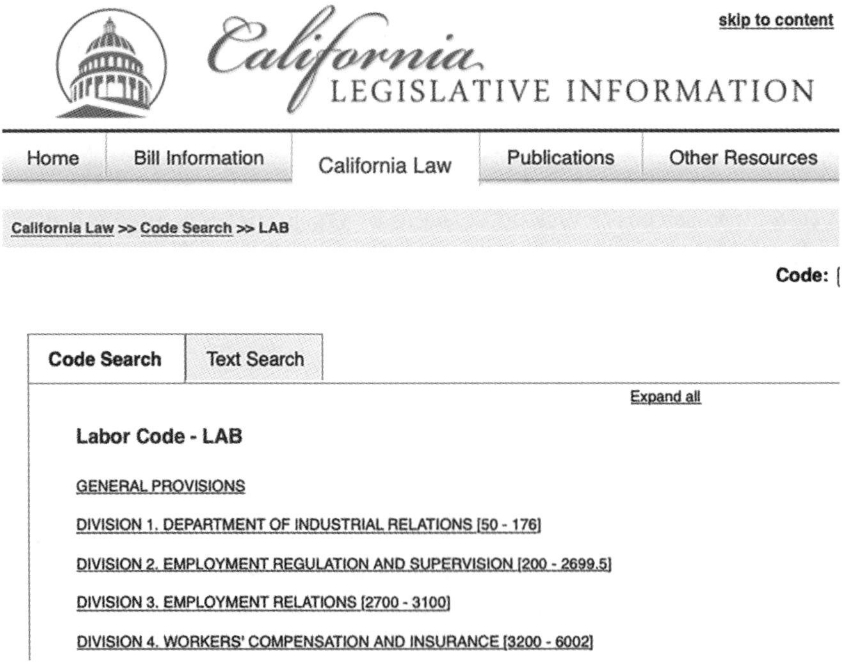

Source: California Legislative Information, at leginfo.legislature.ca.gov/faces/codes.xhtml (click on "Labor Code — LAB").

C. Natural-Language Searching

Natural-language search engines allow searches that use a simple question, phrase, or word. These search engines are designed to produce a list of results and to rank the value of the results. A natural-language search for the project in Chapter 1, for a researcher who does not know the cause of action, is *sue driver who injured wife causing husband emotional trauma*. On Westlaw or Lexis, this search produces an excellent list of authorities. On less advanced services, natural-language searching might produce only limited results, so caution is advised.

1. Natural-Language Searching on Westlaw and Lexis

Westlaw and Lexis have sophisticated search engines that are designed for natural-language searching. With each of these services, you type search terms into a general search bar. An added benefit of Westlaw and Lexis is that their algorithms look for not only the exact terms in your search but also related terms. For example, in researching *negligent infliction of emotional distress*, a cause of action related to the project in Chapter 1, you could enter *NIED* and Westlaw would return cases that included not only that abbreviation but also the full term *negligent infliction of emotional distress*.

Before searching, you can limit the results you retrieve. You can limit by jurisdiction (e.g., searching only California materials), by the category of document (e.g., cases, statutes), or by the type of law addressed in the documents (e.g., criminal law, torts). You can then narrow the search results even further by using filters. Common filters allow you to restrict your search by court (e.g., intermediate or highest appellate court), by date (e.g., only results after a certain year), or by terms (e.g., looking only for arson involving schools).

2. Natural-Language Searching with Other Online Services

Some online services do not provide natural-language searching. Even when it is an option, natural language is not a comprehensive way to search with less sophisticated search engines. Many researchers use this approach just to begin searching on those services. Once they find a case that is on point, however, they refine their search using terms-and-connectors techniques, which are explained later in this chapter, or digests, which are explained in Chapter 4.

One of the difficulties of natural-language searching is that it can produce lists of documents that are not very relevant to your research. This result may either mean that no better matches exist, or it may mean that you did not craft the search carefully enough. Some services' natural-language programs are set to retrieve a particular number of results; retrieving 100 documents does not mean that those 100 documents are all relevant. On the other hand, sometimes the best hit from your perspective will not even appear on the first screen of results, so skimming through the results is always very important.

D. Terms-and-Connectors Searching

A more precise way of searching online uses terms and connectors. Terms-and-connectors searches use connecting symbols to dictate where search terms should be in relation to each other in the documents retrieved. Most services allow terms-and-connectors searching, although their connectors vary. An outline of the steps to constructing an effective search is provided in Table 2-3.

Table 2-3. Outline for Constructing Terms-and-Connectors Searches

1. Generate search terms, then modify them with expanders and placeholders.
2. Add connectors.
3. Choose the appropriate sources or databases to search.
4. Use relevant segments or fields to restrict the search by date, court, judge, or other option.
5. Refine the search, as needed, based on the results.

1. Generate Search Terms

Generate a comprehensive list of search terms, following the suggestions in Chapter 1. This step is critically important with less sophisticated search engines that are very literal. If the author of a particular document did not use the exact term you are searching for, that document will not appear in your results.

Next, modify the search terms with expanders and placeholders so that a search will find variations of your words. The exclamation point typically expands words beyond a common root. For example, *employ!* will find employee, employer, employed, employs, employing, etc. The asterisk or a question mark may serve as a placeholder for an individual letter. On some services, up to three asterisks can be used in a single term. This symbol is helpful when you are not sure which form of the word is used, or when you are not sure of the spelling of a word. For example, the search term *dr*nk* will find drink, drank, and drunk. Placeholders are preferable to the expander in some instances. Using an expander on *trad!* with hopes of finding *trade, trading, trades*, etc. will also produce results that include *traditional*. A better search term may be *trad****.

2. Add Connectors

Connectors determine where search terms will be placed in relation to one another in targeted documents. Effective use of connectors is critical in finding relevant authority. Even minimally sophisticated combinations of the various connectors and commands can make your searches much more effective. Table 2-4 summarizes the most common connectors. Review the specific connectors on each search engine you use before beginning your research. You can find lists of the connectors on Westlaw and Lexis by clicking on "Advanced."

Note the following example of a search for determining whether an employer can prevent a former employee from working for a competitor or starting a new, competing business: *(covenant or contract) /p (noncompetition or*

Table 2-4. Connectors and Commands

Goal	Common Connectors and Commands
Find alternative terms anywhere in the document	or blank space
Find both terms anywhere in the document	and &
Find both terms within a particular distance from each other	/s or S/ = in 1 sentence /x or N/x = within x words
Find terms used as a phrase	put the phrase in quotation marks
Control the hierarchy of searching	parentheses
Exclude terms	and not but not % NOT
Extend the end of a term	!
Hold the place of letters in a term	* ?

"restraint of trade") /p employ! This search will look for paragraphs that contain either of the terms *(covenant or contract)*, and either of the terms *(noncompetition or "restraint of trade")*, and variations of the terms *employ, employee, employer, employment,* etc. Without the parentheses, the search may treat the example as a request for any one of the following three options: (1) the word *covenant*; (2) *contract* within the same paragraph as *noncompetition*; or (3) the phrase *"restraint of trade"* within the same paragraph as variations of *employ, employee,* etc.

3. Choose Sources or Databases

Terms-and-connectors searches are typically conducted in the full text of documents to look for exact matches. Thus, to begin searching in a service with multiple databases (also called "sources"), you must choose which subset of that provider's sources to search. Your research will be more efficient if you restrict each search to the smallest subset of documents that will contain the documents needed. In addition, searches in the smaller subsets are typically less expensive than searches in vast databases. Use larger databases only if searches produce no or few results, or later in your research to ensure you have been comprehensive.

Most services have directories to allow you to browse among the sources and databases that are available for research. Clicking on the "i" next to the name of a source or database will provide information about its scope. Note that the list of sources or databases shown on a particular page may not include all that are available.

4. Restrict the Search with "Fields" and "Segments"

With terms-and-connectors searching, some services allow you to search specific parts of documents, such as the date, author, or court. On Westlaw, they are called *fields* and are available using the "Advanced" search option. On Lexis, these specific parts are called document *segments*; you can learn more about them by clicking on "Tips."

Two examples demonstrate the usefulness of segment and field searching. First, in conducting a full-text search, you can ensure that the results directly address your topic by searching the syllabi or synopses of the documents. Because this segment or field summarizes the contents of the document, your terms will appear there only if they are the focus of the document. Thus, the search will weed out documents where your terms are mentioned only in passing or in a footnote. Second, if you know the author of a relevant opinion or article, you can search for her name in the appropriate segment or field, eliminating documents where the person is referred to only tangentially or is cited in a footnote.

5. Refine or Broaden the Search

With a query of terms and connectors, a search may result in a reasonable number of highly relevant documents, or no documents, or more than 1,000 documents. In the latter two instances, refining the search is necessary. When a search produces no results, try one of the following:

- use broader connectors (e.g., search for terms in the same paragraph rather than in the same sentence);
- use more general terms (e.g., search for *spouse* rather than *wife* or *husband*); or
- use a larger set of sources or a larger database (e.g., all California cases, not just Supreme Court cases).

When a search produces a long list of results, skim them to see whether they are on point. If the results seem irrelevant, modify or edit the search query by using more specific terms, more restrictive connectors, or a smaller set of sources or databases. You can also refine your results by using the narrowing function discussed earlier for Westlaw and Lexis.

E. Topic Searching Online

Sophisticated online search engines and services have tools for topic searching. The most user-friendly of these tools allow the researcher to begin with a list of broad areas of law and narrow the topic by clicking through successive lists.

Using Lexis, for example, click on "Browse" at the top of the page and then "Topics"; you can either select one of the topics listed or enter search terms in a box. If you select one of the topics (e.g., "Workers' Compensation"), you will be able to open its subtopics and eventually "Get topic documents" using a drop-down menu. If instead you enter search terms, the results will show how many hits appear in each of the topics listed on the initial page. You can open each topic and review the subtopics that contain your search terms. Again, clicking on the subtopics will allow you to select "Get topic documents." Under either approach, you can filter the resulting documents using the techniques discussed earlier.

F. Working with Online Documents

In most online services, you can move through a document either by scrolling through screens or by clicking through search terms. If the search term feature is not available, try using the "Find" feature on your web browser. Some services allow for book browsing, so that you can see the previous or next page of a set of documents. Reviewing nearby pages through book browsing can help provide context.

One advantage to working in the premier services is the ability to highlight, annotate, and save documents in a system of folders (sometimes called a "workspace"). After creating folders and adding documents to them, some services allow you to access the folders and documents from any computer or mobile device and to share folders with co-workers.

G. Printing, Downloading, or Emailing Results

Westlaw and Lexis allow you to print, download, or email documents in addition to saving them to folders. Some researchers choose to read and organize research documents entirely on the computer. However, many researchers still find it easier to read documents carefully on paper as opposed to the computer screen, and some prefer having key authorities in print on their desks rather than saved as separate files on their computer. Given the cost and environmental impact of printing, you should exercise caution in deciding which documents are truly needed in print.

H. Keeping Track

Many online services provide lists of past searches and results, and you should form the habit of printing or saving them. Westlaw and Lexis both provide "History" links that store your searches and results for periods ranging from three months to a year. The "History" link is available at the top right of every screen.

Chapter 11 of this book offers suggestions for keeping track of your research process and the documents that it produces. You might want to take a look at that chapter now, even though some of the details may not be clear until you have read the intervening chapters.

II. Other Online Research Services

Westlaw and Lexis are still the premier online tools for legal research because they provide the most documents and the most advanced search techniques. Bloomberg Law is increasing its content and functionality, although it still lags behind the two leaders in some respects. Currently, its real edge is in transactional research and in court dockets.

Other providers offer services that might suit your needs. Often these other online services provide more limited content, but at more economical prices. Three of these fee-based services are Fastcase, Casemaker, and VersusLaw. Their search mechanisms tend to be less user-friendly, but their prices are lower. VersusLaw, for example, offers an inexpensive monthly plan that includes federal and state materials and a basic citator service. Some state bar associations make either Casemaker or Fastcase available for free to their members, although California does not.

One helpful online site with free material for anyone is Google Scholar. It provides access to state and federal cases, as well as law review articles. There is a rudimentary citator, *How cited*, but the site does not currently include statutes, regulations, or other legal documents.

Remember that each online provider might have its own unique search techniques or commands. Reviewing a "help" or "tips" link is usually the best place to begin working with an unfamiliar service.

III. Print Research Techniques

Today, fewer researchers approach legal problems with a firm foundation in print research techniques. While the vast quantity of information available online has decreased the demand for print sources, not all legal material is available online. Even when sources are available both online and in print, print sources are sometimes more efficient to use. The efficiency may be simply because a library has already paid for the sources and provides them for free, or because the organization of a source is more apparent in print format.

Locating print sources in a library may require using an online catalog of the library's holdings. These catalogs are usually easy to navigate, but reference librarians can provide assistance. Librarians might even suggest specific titles or areas of the library with relevant sources.

As with online research, the table of contents is an important guide to see how a print resource is organized and to find relevant sections. Scan the table of contents for your research terms, recognizing that you may be referred to relevant pages, section numbers, or paragraph numbers, depending on how that source is organized.

The index—the alphabetical listing of topics included in a book or series of books—is a frequent starting point for researching in print resources. Often, it is wise to spend some time in the index looking for several of your research terms to ensure that you begin your research in the most helpful part of the volume, not just the part you encountered first. An index will often contain cross-references to other entries. Take a few moments to learn the cross-reference signals of a new book, as they vary among resources. In multi-volume series, the index is likely to be located in the last volume. Separate indexes may be provided for each volume or for each legal topic.

Chapter 3

Judicial Opinions[1]

Although case law is at the bottom of the hierarchy of primary authority, the ultimate goal of much legal research is to find cases that have interpreted and applied constitutions, statutes, and regulations or created common law. Thus, this book begins to explore primary authority with a discussion of judicial opinions — informally called cases — so you can better understand how to research the other sources of law discussed in succeeding chapters.

Courts write judicial opinions to explain their decisions in litigated disputes. Cases are published in chronological order in books called *reporters*. Reporters are fundamental tools of legal research, regardless of whether a researcher is using online or print sources, because cases are most often identified by their print reporter citations even by online services. Some reporters include only cases decided by a certain court, for example, the California Supreme Court. Other reporters include cases from courts within a specific geographic region, for example, the western United States.[2]

Following an overview of the California and federal court systems, this chapter explains reporters and the features added to opinions when they are published in reporters. The chapter ends with suggestions for reading cases effectively. The next chapter discusses case law research.

---

1. Portions of this chapter are drawn from *Oregon Legal Research* by Suzanne E. Rowe and are used with permission.

2. Still other reporters publish only those cases that deal with a certain topic, such as bankruptcy.

Table 3-1. Districts of the California Courts of Appeal

District	Headquarters
First Appellate District*	San Francisco
Second Appellate District*	Los Angeles
Third Appellate District	Sacramento
Fourth Appellate District*	San Diego
Fifth Appellate District	Fresno
Sixth Appellate District	San Jose

* These three districts are subdivided into divisions.

I. Court Systems

The basic court structure includes a trial court, an intermediate appellate court, and an ultimate appellate court, often called the "supreme" court.[3] These courts exist at both the state and federal levels.[4]

A. California Courts

The trial courts of California are called *superior courts*. There is a superior court in each of the state's fifty-eight counties. Most counties have multiple court locations, resulting in more than 450 trial court locations around the state. Most of the cases in the state system begin in a superior court. These courts hear cases concerning civil, criminal, family, probate, and juvenile matters.[5]

The state's intermediate courts are called *courts of appeal*. The state is divided into six appellate districts. The headquarters of the six districts are provided in Table 3-1. The California Courts of Appeal have appellate jurisdiction over

---

3. The following discussion omits tribal courts in California. Information is available at courts.ca.gov/programs-tribal.htm.

4. Most states have an intermediate appellate court, but a handful of states with smaller populations do not. Moreover, in some state systems the highest court is not called the "supreme" court. In New York, for example, the "Court of Appeals" is the highest court, and the trial court is called the "Supreme Court."

5. Prior to 1998, California trial courts were divided into superior and municipal courts. Following a constitutional amendment, trial courts were able to unify into superior courts that hear all types of cases. Each of the fifty-eight counties has now moved to the unified system.

cases decided by the superior courts and by certain administrative agencies. They have original jurisdiction in a few areas, such as habeas corpus.

California's highest court is the California Supreme Court, which is located in San Francisco, although it regularly hears cases in Los Angeles and Sacramento. The California Supreme Court has seven justices. It has discretion to review cases decided by the courts of appeal, and it exercises that discretion to hear only cases involving significant questions of law or uniform application of the law. This court must, however, hear cases involving the death penalty.

Cases decided by the California Supreme Court are mandatory authority in all lower courts in the state. Cases decided by any of the six courts of appeal are mandatory authority in all superior courts, whether or not the superior court is in the geographical district of a particular court of appeal. Because decisions of one court of appeal are not binding on the other five courts of appeal, it is possible to find conflicting decisions among the six districts. In those instances, superior courts may follow the decision of any court of appeal,[6] but as a practical matter most follow the decision of the court of appeal in whose district the superior court sits.[7] Eventually, the California Supreme Court is likely to resolve the conflict by granting review in a case addressing the issue.

Cases decided by the California Supreme Court are heard by all seven of the sitting justices, unless a justice is recused from a particular case. Cases decided by the California Courts of Appeal are heard by three justices sitting as a *panel* of the full court.[8] A party who does not agree with the decision of a panel may ask for a rehearing *en banc*, meaning that all of the justices on that court would rehear the case.

The California courts' website at courts.ca.gov provides information about the courts, their jurisdiction, their locations, their calendars, and much more. The link "About California Courts" is a good place to begin.

---

6. *Auto Equity Sales, Inc. v. Superior Court of Santa Clara Cty.*, 57 Cal. 2d 450, 456 (1962).

7. *McCallum v. McCallum*, 190 Cal. App. 3d 308, 315 n.4 (1987).

8. Jurists on most intermediate appellate courts are called "Judges," but California uses the term "Justices."

B. Federal Courts

In the federal judicial system, the trial courts are called United States District Courts. There are ninety-four district courts in the federal system, with each district contained in a particular state. California is divided into four federal districts: northern, central, southern, and eastern. Among western states, only California and Washington have more than one federal district. The entire state of Oregon, for example, makes up the federal District of Oregon. Similarly, Arizona, Nevada, Utah, and other western states have just one federal district.

The federal system's intermediate appellate courts are called United States Courts of Appeals. The country is divided into thirteen federal circuits.[9] California is in the Ninth Circuit, so cases from the United States District Courts in California are appealed to the United States Court of Appeals for the Ninth Circuit. This circuit encompasses Alaska, Arizona, California, Hawaii, Idaho, Montana, Nevada, Oregon, and Washington, as well as Guam and the Northern Mariana Islands.

The highest court in the federal system is the United States Supreme Court, which is the final arbiter of federal law (e.g., the United States Constitution and federal statutes). This Court has discretionary review, meaning parties must petition to have cases heard.

As in the California court system, decisions of the highest court in the federal system are mandatory authority in all federal courts below it (and on state courts hearing issues of federal law). Unlike the California system, however, decisions of the intermediate courts of appeals are mandatory authority in trial courts within only that circuit. For example, a decision of the Ninth Circuit Court of Appeals is mandatory authority in district courts in California but only persuasive authority in district courts in Virginia, which is in the Fourth Circuit.

The website for the federal judiciary is uscourts.gov.

---

9. A map showing the federal circuits and linking to their websites is available at uscourts.gov/about-federal-courts/federal-courts-public/court-website-links.

II. Reporters

Even though attorneys usually read cases online, convention calls for citation to reporters (i.e., books containing the cases), and an understanding of the reporter system is essential to lawyering success.

A. Reporters for California Cases

The California Constitution requires that all opinions issued by the California Supreme Court be published. The official reporter (i.e., the reporter published by, or under contract with, the state) for these cases is *California Reports*. California Court of Appeal opinions are published in a separate official reporter called *California Appellate Reports*. Only a small percentage of court of appeal decisions are published. For instance, only eight percent of the nearly 10,000 California appellate opinions issued in 2015–2016 were published.[10] Opinions that are not published in *California Appellate Reports* are considered "unpublished" and may not be cited and generally should not be used in any manner.[11] Cases from state trial courts in California are not published; in fact, few states publish opinions at the trial court level. Unpublished opinions may be obtained directly from the California court that decided the case but may not be cited to or used as authority.

California Reports and *California Appellate Reports* are the official reporters for California. Cases from California's appellate courts are also reported in two unofficial reporters. California Supreme Court cases are published in West's *Pacific Reporter* and in *West's California Reporter*. Since 1960, California Court of Appeal cases have appeared in *West's California Reporter*, not *Pacific Reporter*.

---

10. See information at courts.ca.gov/documents/2017-Court-Statistics-Report.pdf.

11. Cal. R. Ct. 8.1115. Even among the published court of appeal decisions, some have been "depublished." In the past, when the California Supreme Court accepted a case for review, the appellate court decision was automatically "depublished." The effect was the same as if the decision had never been published—it was generally unciteable. This rule changed in 2016, so California appellate decisions now remain published and citable even after the Supreme Court accepts review. *See* Cal. R. Ct. 8.1105. However, these court of appeal cases have no precedential weight while they are under review by the Supreme Court. After the Supreme Court issues its decision, the appellate opinion regains precedential weight only to the extent it is consistent with the Supreme Court's decision. The Supreme Court can also order depublication of a court of appeal opinion either upon the request of a party or when the Supreme Court disagrees with the reasoning of the opinion. In these instances, the depublished case will remain on Lexis and Westlaw and in unofficial reporters, but not in *California Appellate Reports*.

Table 3-2. Reporters for California Appellate Cases*

Court	Reporter Name	Abbreviation
California Supreme Court	California Reports (official)	Cal., Cal. 2d, Cal. 3d, Cal. 4th, Cal. 5th
	Pacific Reporter	P., P.2d, P.3d
	West's California Reporter	Cal. Rptr., Cal. Rptr. 2d, Cal. Rptr. 3d
California Courts of Appeal	California Appellate Reports (official)	Cal. App., Cal. App. 2d, Cal. App. 3d, Cal. App. 4th, Cal. App. 5th
	Pacific Reporter (through 1959)	P., P.2d, P.3d
	West's California Reporter (since 1960)	Cal. Rptr., Cal. Rptr. 2d, Cal. Rptr. 3d

* Some opinions of the Superior Court Appellate Division are published in a separate section of *California Appellate Reports*.

While the text of the court's opinion is the same in the official and unofficial reporters, the appearance, pagination, and editorial additions are different. Table 3-2 lists the various reporters for California's appellate cases.

Commercial reporters often combine several courts' opinions under a single title. *Pacific Reporter* publishes cases from the courts of the following fifteen states: Alaska, Arizona, California, Colorado, Hawaii, Idaho, Kansas, Montana, Nevada, New Mexico, Oklahoma, Oregon, Utah, Washington, and Wyoming.[12] *Pacific Reporter* includes cases from the intermediate and highest appellate courts of most of these states. The other regional reporters are *North Eastern Reporter*, *Atlantic Reporter*, *South Eastern Reporter*, *Southern Reporter*, *South Western Reporter*, and *North Western Reporter*. All of these regional reporters are published by West. Because the publisher decided which states to group together in regional reporters, these groupings have no legal significance. Moreover, the coverage of each regional reporter is not the same as the composition of the federal circuits.

Reporters are published in *series*. Cases currently being published in *California Reports* and *California Appellate Reports* are appearing in the fifth series. *Pacific Reporter* and *West's California Reporter* are each in the third series. To find a case in a reporter with multiple series, whether searching in print or

---

12. If a state does not publish its own reporter, the regional reporter may be the official reporter. For example, the official reporter of Alaska cases is *Pacific Reporter*.

online, you must know the series in which the case was reported. This information is included in the citation to the case, as explained below.

You can also find cases online, both via paid subscription services and free research websites, as discussed in more detail in the next chapter. Online cases retain the editorial features and citation conventions of their hard copy predecessors.

1. Citing California Cases

A citation to a California case requires the names of the parties, the volume and abbreviation for the reporter, the initial page of the case, and the year the case was decided.[13] *California Reports* is abbreviated as "Cal." The case *People v. Davis*, 18 Cal. 4th 712 (1998), can be found in volume 18 of the fourth series of *California Reports*, starting on page 712. The case was decided in 1998. The abbreviation for *California Appellate Reports* is "Cal. App." The case *McBride v. Smith*, 18 Cal. App. 5th 1160 (2018), was published in volume 18 of the fifth series of *California Appellate Reports*, beginning on page 1160. It was decided in 2018.

In California, all documents submitted to a California court must cite the official reporters (Cal. and Cal. App.).[14] For documents that are not going to be submitted to a California court, lawyers usually follow the custom of their firm or office. Especially when writing a memo for a firm outside of California, you would likely cite California cases to *Pacific Reporter*. When citing to a regional reporter, always indicate the state court name within a parenthetical.

EXAMPLES: *People v. Davis*, 958 P.2d 1083 (Cal. 1998).

State v. Vallin, 434 P.3d 413 (Or. 2019).

2. Features of a Reported Case

The following discussion relates to cases published on Westlaw, in *West's California Reporter*, or in *Pacific Reporter*. Knowing how West organizes its cases will also provide you with the tools to understand what you see in a case published by a different publisher.

---

13. The following citations adhere to the practitioner citation format of the *ALWD Guide*, which is identical to the practitioner citation format used under the *Bluebook*. For academic citation formats under the *ALWD Guide* and the *Bluebook*, as well as formats adhering to the *California Style Manual*, see Chapter 12.

14. Cal. R. Ct. 3.1113(c).

A case printed in a reporter, or viewed on Westlaw or Lexis, contains the exact language of the court's opinion. Additionally, the publisher includes supplemental information to aid researchers in learning about the case, locating the relevant parts of the case, and finding similar cases. Some of these research aids are gleaned from the court record of the case, while others are written by the publisher's editorial staff. Most reporters will include these items, though perhaps in a different order, and they will look slightly different when viewed online rather than in books. To best understand the following discussion, refer to the *West's California Reporter* excerpt of *People v. Davis* in Figure 3-1. Westlaw and Lexis images of the same case are available at the end of the chapter in Appendix 3-A and 3-B.

Parallel citation. The reporter provides the citation for the case in any official or other unofficial reporter in which the case is also printed.

Parties and procedural designations. Most reported cases are from appellate courts. The appealing party is called the *appellant*; the other party is the *respondent.*[15]

Docket number. The docket number is a series of letters and numbers assigned by a court for keeping track of documents pertaining to a particular case. A case will have a different docket number in each court that hears the case.

Deciding court. The opinion gives the full name of the court that decided the case. For cases from the courts of appeal, this information includes both the district and, where appropriate, the division.

Date of decision. Each case begins with the date the case was argued and submitted to the court, and the date of the court's decision. For citation purposes, only the year the case was decided is important.

Synopsis. The synopsis is a short summary of the key facts, procedure, legal points, and disposition of the case. Reading a synopsis can quickly tell you whether a case is on point. You cannot rely exclusively on a synopsis and you must never cite it, but it is a very useful research tool.

Disposition. The disposition of the case is the appellate court's decision to affirm, reverse, remand, or vacate the decision below. If the appellate court agrees with only part of the lower court's decision, the appellate court may affirm in part and reverse in part.

---

15. In most jurisdictions, the terms appellant-appellee are used when a party has a right to appeal, while the terms petitioner-respondent apply to parties when the court has discretion to hear the appeal. California uses the term respondent for the non-moving party in both instances.

Figure 3-1. Case Excerpt in West Reporter

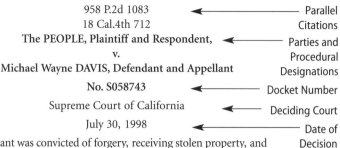

958 P.2d 1083 ⟵ Parallel
18 Cal.4th 712 Citations

The PEOPLE, Plaintiff and Respondent, ⟵ Parties and
v. Procedural
Michael Wayne DAVIS, Defendant and Appellant Designations

No. S058743 ⟵ Docket Number

Supreme Court of California ⟵ Deciding Court

July 30, 1998 ⟵ Date of
Decision

Defendant was convicted of forgery, receiving stolen property, and
burglary following jury trial in the Superior Court, Sonoma County,
No. SCR22933, George L. Nelson, Retired Judge of the Justice
Court, sitting by assignment. Defendant appealed, and the Court
of Appeal affirmed. The Supreme Court granted review, superseding
the opinion of the Court of Appeal, and held in an opinion by
George, C.J., that placing a forged check in a chute in the walk-up ⟵ Synopsis
window of a check-cashing facility, or inserting a stolen ATM card
into an ATM, is not an "entry" for purposes of the burglary statute,
disapproving *People v. Ravenscroft*, 198 Cal.App.3d 639, 243
Cal.Rptr. 827.

Judgment of Court of Appeal affirmed in part, reversed in part. ⟵ Disposition

Baxter, J., filed a dissenting opinion in which Chin and Brown,
JJ., Joined.

Opinion, 59 Cal.Rptr.2d 584, vacated.

1. **Burglary** 🗝 9(2)
   Passing forged check through a chute in a walk-up window of
   a check-cashing facility, or inserting stolen automated teller
   machine (ATM) card into an ATM, is not an "entry" within the ⟵ Headnote
   meaning of the burglary statute; although intended result in
   each instance is larceny, neither act violates occupant's possessory interest in building as does using a tool to reach into a
   building and remove property; disapproving People v. Ravenscroft, 198 Cal.App.3d 639, 243 Cal.Rptr. 827. West's Ann.Cal.
   Penal Code § 459.

2. **Burglary** 🗝 2
   Burglary may be committed by using an instrument to enter
   a building, whether that instrument is used solely to effect
   entry, or to accomplish the intended larceny or felony as well.
   West's Ann.Cal.Penal Code § 459.

Headnotes. A headnote is a sentence or short paragraph provided by the publisher that sets out a single point of law in a case. Most cases will have several headnotes, and some have many headnotes. The text of headnotes often comes directly from the language of the opinion. Even so, you must cite only to the opinion, which you can do easily as the headnotes are hyperlinked to the opinion.

Just after the headnote number, each headnote begins with a word or phrase and a number. On Westlaw and in West reporters, these are called *topics* and *key numbers*, which are used in subject indexes to locate other cases that discuss similar points of law. These subject indexes, called *digests*, are discussed in Chapter 4.

Procedural information. *West's California Reporter* volumes contain some procedural information, such as the court from which the case was appealed and the justice who wrote the decision. Note that following a justice's name will be "C.J." for the chief justice (or "P.J." for the presiding justice in the Court of Appeal) or "J." for another justice. If a case includes concurring or dissenting opinions, they will be noted in the procedural listings with their authors and the names of any justices who joined those opinions. This section also provides the names of the attorneys who argued for each party.

Opinion. In *West's California Reporter*, the actual opinion of the court begins immediately following the name of the justice who wrote the opinion. If the justices who heard the case do not agree on the outcome or the reasons for the outcome, there may be several opinions:

- *Majority opinion*: The opinion supported by a majority of the justices.
- *Concurring opinion*: An opinion that agrees with the outcome but not the reasoning of the majority.
- *Dissenting opinion*: An opinion written by a justice who disagrees with the outcome supported by the majority of the justices.

Other justices may join with the author of a concurring or dissenting opinion. While only the majority opinion is binding on future courts, the other opinions provide valuable insights and may be cited as persuasive authority. If there is no majority on both the outcome and the reasoning, the case will be decided by whichever opinion garners the most support, which is called a *plurality decision*. As a final alternative, a *per curiam* decision is issued by the court as a whole; no single justice is given authorship credit.

3. Other Sources for California Cases

A *slip opinion* is the actual document produced by the court, without the editorial enhancements normally added by the publisher. California Supreme Court cases are posted immediately upon filing. California Court of Appeal opinions are routinely posted within a few hours of filing and may be filed any time during the day. Slip opinions are available either from the court that decided the case or online at courts.ca.gov/opinions.

In addition, cases are added daily to Lexis and Westlaw. Checking those websites is often the fastest way to find a new opinion, particularly one from a state other than California that may not post opinions as quickly.

Table 3-3. Reporters for Federal Court Cases

Court	Reporter Name	Abbreviation
U.S. Supreme Court	*United States Reports* (official)	U.S.
	Supreme Court Reporter	S. Ct.
	United States Supreme Court Reports, Lawyers' Edition	L. Ed., L. Ed. 2d
U.S. Courts of Appeals	*Federal Reporter*	F., F.2d, F.3d
U.S. District Courts	*Federal Supplement*	F. Supp., F. Supp. 2d, F. Supp. 3d

B. Reporters for Federal Cases

Reporters are also published for cases decided by federal courts. Table 3-3 lists the federal court reporters, along with their citation abbreviations.

Decisions of the United States Supreme Court are reported in *United States Reports* (official); *Supreme Court Reporter* (West); and *United States Supreme Court Reports, Lawyers' Edition* (Lexis). Although the official *United States Reports* should be cited if possible, that series frequently does not publish cases until several years after they are decided. Thus, for recent cases, lawyers often cite *Supreme Court Reporter*.

Cases decided by the federal intermediate appellate courts are published in *Federal Reporter*, now in its third series. Some United States Courts of Appeals cases that are not published in *Federal Reporter*, and therefore are not precedential, may be found in *Federal Appendix*. Selected cases from the United States District Courts, the federal trial courts, are reported in *Federal Supplement*, which is also in its third series. The West reporter *Federal Rules Decisions* publishes select district court cases that interpret federal rules, such as the Federal Rules of Criminal, Civil, or Appellate Procedure.

Federal cases are available online, with Supreme Court cases available most readily. The Court's website at supremecourt.gov includes slip opinions soon after the decisions are rendered, as well as opinions from 1991 to the present. Limited access to court of appeals and district court cases may be available from the individual court's website. An educational site supported by Cornell University also provides federal cases quickly; the address is law.cornell.edu/supct/. Lexis and Westlaw publish federal opinions soon after they are released. Remember that both services also make available "unpublished" opinions. Check court rules to determine the weight each court gives to unpublished opinions before citing one.

III. Reading and Analyzing Cases

Reading a case and analyzing its potential relevance to the problem you are researching can be challenging, time-consuming work. Lawyers spend hours reading (and re-reading) cases, especially in unfamiliar areas of law, when they may need to refer frequently to a law dictionary to try to understand the terms used. Using the following strategies should make reading and analyzing cases more effective.

A. Reading Cases Effectively

You should read a case at least three times before using it in your analysis: (1) to determine whether it is relevant; (2) to understand the case; and (3) to take notes on how it applies to your research problem.

First, review the synopsis quickly to determine whether the case seems relevant to your problem. If it does, skim the headnotes to find the particular portion of the case that is relevant. Go directly to the portion of the case identified by the relevant headnote or headnotes, skipping other portions initially, and decide whether the case is important for your project. If it is relevant, skim the entire case to understand what happened and why. You should still be focusing on the portion of the case identified by the relevant headnote or headnotes, but you need the context of the entire case.

Second, after determining that a case is relevant, read the case slowly and carefully to understand its facts, analysis, and outcome. At the end of each paragraph or page, consider what you have read. If you cannot summarize the concepts, try reading the material again.

Read the case a third time, this time taking notes. The notes may be as formal as a "case brief" or as informal as a list of points. Regardless of the form, the process of taking notes will help you parse, identify, and comprehend the essential concepts of the case. If you have to write a legal document about your research problem, the notes will help you organize your analysis into an outline.

B. Analyzing the Substance of Cases

If a case involves legally significant facts that are similar to your client's situation and the court applies law on point for your problem, then the case is relevant and you should carefully consider the case as you analyze your problem. Legally significant facts are those that affect the court's decision. Some attorneys call these determinative facts. Which facts are legally significant depends on the case. Facts about the condition of the defendant's tires or the defendant's medical records are likely irrelevant in a corporate law dispute, but highly relevant in a vehicular manslaughter case.

Even with the most thorough research, you are unlikely to find a case whose facts are identical to those of your client. Rather, you will find cases with more similar or less similar facts. Your job is to determine whether the case's facts are similar enough to your client's facts for the court to apply the law in the same way and reach the same result. If the outcome of the decided case favors your client's position, you will highlight the similarities. If the outcome of the decided case is not favorable from your client's perspective, you may argue that the case is distinguishable based on those factual differences, or you may argue that the reasoning of the decided case is faulty. Remember that you have an ethical duty to ensure that the court knows about a case directly on point from the controlling jurisdiction, even if the outcome of that case is adverse to your client.

It is also unlikely that one case will address all aspects of your client's situation. Most legal claims have several elements or factors. *Elements* are required subparts of a claim; *factors* are important considerations, no one of which will decide the case. If a court decides that one element is not met, it might not discuss the others. In a different case, the court may decide that two factors are so overwhelming that the others have no impact on the outcome. In these circumstances, you would have to find other cases that analyze the remaining elements or factors.

After determining that a case is relevant to some portion of your analysis, you must decide how heavily that case will weigh in your analysis. You need to consider two important points here. One is the concept of *stare decisis*; the other is the difference between the *holding* of the case and *dicta* within that case.

Stare decisis means "to stand by things decided." This concept means that courts must follow prior opinions, ensuring consistency in the application of the law. *Stare decisis*, however, is limited to the courts within one jurisdiction. The Courts of Appeal of California must follow the decisions of the California Supreme Court but not those of the courts of any other state. The concept of *stare decisis* also applies to a court with respect to its own opinions. The California Supreme Court, thus, should follow its own earlier cases in deciding new matters. If a court decides not to continue following its earlier cases, it is usually because of changes in society that have outdated the law of the earlier case or because a new statute has been enacted that changes the legal landscape.

Under *stare decisis*, courts are required to follow the *holding* of prior cases. The *holding* is the court's ultimate decision on the matter of law at issue in the case. Other statements or observations included in the opinion are not binding; they are referred to as *dicta*. For example, in deciding whether passing a bad check through the window at a bank's drive-through facility was burglary, a court observed that such a holding would mean a person putting his arm through a library chute to remove books would commit burglary. That observation was based on hypothetical facts and was not the basis of the court's decision. The observation is therefore dicta and is not binding on future courts, though it may be cited as persuasive authority.

After finding a number of relevant cases, you must synthesize them to state and explain the legal rule. Sometimes a court states the rule fully; if not, you must piece together the information from relevant cases. Then use the analysis and facts of various cases to explain the law. Decide how the rule applies to the client's facts, and determine your conclusion. Note that this method of synthesis is much more than mere summaries of all the various cases followed by a summary of your client's facts.

Appendix 3-A. Case Excerpt on Westlaw Edge

View Cal./Cal.App. version

18 Cal.4th 712
Supreme Court of California

The PEOPLE, Plaintiff and Respondent,
v.
Michael Wayne DAVIS, Defendant and Appellant.

No. S058743.
July 30, 1998.

Synopsis

Defendant was convicted of forgery, receiving stolen property, and burglary following jury trial in the Superior Court, Sonoma County, No. SCR22933, George L. Nelson, Retired Judge of the Justice Court, sitting by assignment. Defendant appealed, and The Court of Appeal affirmed. The Supreme Court granted review, superseding the opinion of the Court of Appeal, and held in an opinion by George, C.J., that placing a forged check in a chute in the walk-up window of a check-cashing facility, or inserting a stolen ATM card into an ATM, is not an "entry" for purposes of the burglary statute, disapproving ⚑ *People v. Ravenscroft*, 198 Cal.App.3d 639, 243 Cal.Rptr. 827.

Judgment of Court of Appeal affirmed in part, reversed in part.

Baxter, J., filed a dissenting opinion in which Chin and Brown, JJ., joined.

Opinion, ⚑ 59 Cal.Rptr.2d 584, vacated.

Source: Westlaw. Used with permission of Thomson Reuters.

Appendix 3-B. Case Excerpt on Lexis Advance®

 People v. Davis, 18 Cal. 4th 712

> **Copy Citation**

Supreme Court of California

July 30, 1998, Decided ; July 30, 1998

No. S058743.

Reporter
18 Cal. 4th 712 * | 958 P.2d 1083 ** | 76 Cal. Rptr. 2d 770 *** | 1998 Cal. LEXIS 4686 **** | 98 Daily Journal DAR 8209 | 98 Cal. Daily Op. Service 5886

THE PEOPLE, Plaintiff and Respondent, v. MICHAEL WAYNE DAVIS, Defendant and Appellant.

Prior History: [****1] Superior Court of Sonoma County. Super. Ct. No. SCR22933. George L. Nelson, Judge.

Disposition: For the reasons discussed above, we conclude that defendant's placement of a forged check in the chute of the walk-up window of the check-cashing facility at issue cannot reasonably be termed an entry into the building for purposes of the burglary statute. Accordingly, the judgment of the Court of Appeal is reversed to the extent it affirms defendant's conviction for burglary, and affirmed in all other respects.

Core Terms

burglary, chute, window, forged check, air space, felony, insertion, burglary statute, card, check-cashing, burglarious entry, burglar, teller, larceny, walk-up, constitutes, purposes, commit, invited, premises, felonious intent, possessory right, forgery, door, burglary conviction, accomplish, enters, stolen, occupant's, physical danger

Case Summary

Procedural Posture
Defendant challenged the evidentiary sufficiency of the judgment of conviction for burglary, entered by the trial court and affirmed by the Court of Appeal (California), based upon evidence that defendant presented a stolen and forged check to the teller at a check-cashing business by placing the check in a chute in a walk-up window. Defendant had also been convicted of forgery and receiving stolen property.

Overview
Defendant was convicted of forgery, under Cal. Penal Code § 470, receiving stolen property under Cal. Penal Code § 469(c), and burglary, under Cal. Penal Code § 459, based upon evidence that he presented a stolen and forged check to the teller at a check-cashing business by placing the check in a chute in a walk-up window. Defendant maintained that the burglary conviction had to be reversed because he did not enter the check-cashing facility. The conviction was affirmed by the lower appellate court. The judgment was reversed. The court determined that the crucial issue was whether this was the type of entry the burglary statute was intended to prevent. The court looked

Chapter 4

Researching Judicial Opinions

The best way to search for judicial opinions is to begin with a case you already have. A case from a supervisor, a colleague, or even an opponent is your best tool for finding more cases. For example, you can

- read the cases cited within that case;
- find later cases that cite back to that case (using the citators explained in Chapter 9);
- find cases sharing your case's key number (explained later in this chapter); and
- find secondary sources that discuss that case.

Without a case as a starting point, most researchers are better off not jumping straight into case law research. It is often preferable to gain some context by beginning with background reading that might allow you to then search for cases more efficiently. For instance, when you are unfamiliar with your client's legal topic, you might run a Google search about the legal issue to gain familiarity with the elements you will see in the case law. Better yet, look in a California-specific secondary source. Witkin's *Summary of California Law* or a Rutter Guide will provide you with an overview of the law — and with a California case citation or two to get you started on your research path. These secondary sources are covered in Chapter 10.

But sometimes attorneys need to *begin* their research by searching for case law. Indeed, attorneys do so every day, especially when working in areas of law that are familiar. For the novice, however, it is important to approach the process of researching judicial opinions with two sobering facts in mind: (1) there are millions of cases already published, with more than a hundred thousand cases decided each year; and (2) the easiest way to find cases is also the most expensive — through the paid subscription services of Westlaw and Lexis. These caveats are especially noteworthy in California, which is a massive jurisdiction. California's court system is one of the largest in the world, and the

California Courts of Appeal issued nearly 23,000 dispositions in 2015–2016 alone.[1]

For these reasons, smart researchers are strategic when researching judicial opinions. This chapter introduces three primary strategies: natural-language searching, terms-and-connectors searching, and digest-based searching. These three strategies are not presented in order of preference. Rather, researchers deploy different strategies at different times depending on their research needs. The chapter concludes with a brief discussion of online paid case law research tools beyond Lexis and Westlaw as well as free sources for case law research.

I. Natural-Language Searching

Natural-language searching is simply the "Google" form of searching that many people do in non-legal contexts: you type terms into a search box and you get results. Yet understanding how this process works in the context of the legal research databases provided by Westlaw and Lexis will make you a smarter—and ultimately more efficient—case law researcher.

With natural-language searches, the formulas that produce results based on your search terms are known as algorithms and are designed by computer scientists at Westlaw and Lexis. While the formulas are proprietary, they are known to include at least the following components: what other attorneys have looked for and ultimately used; the popularity of various terms; synonyms and substitute terms for the requested search terms; and the editorial content of the digest system.[2]

In addition to the general legal research techniques offered in Chapter 2, the following techniques are especially effective for natural-language case law searching:

- Limit the initial search by jurisdiction. In Westlaw, click on "State Materials" and then "California." In Lexis, from the main "Explore Content" page, click on "California." Modify these steps as needed for whichever jurisdiction you are working in.
- Select search terms carefully. Consider putting select terms, such as terms of art, in quotation marks. Examples include "fair use," "adverse possession," and "covenant not to compete."

---

1. See information at courts.ca.gov/documents/2017-Court-Statistics-Report.pdf.
2. The digest system is covered in Part III of this chapter.

- Limit results by cases. For example, after generating results in Westlaw, click on "Cases" on the left-hand side of the page to ensure you are viewing only case law results. In Lexis, from the California page, select a case law-only database such as "California State Cases, Combined."
- Use filters. With filters, you can limit results by court, date, practice area, and publication status, among other helpful criteria. For instance, you can narrow results to only those cases decided by the California Court of Appeal's Third District, or to cases decided since 2010, or to cases that address a specific point of law as identified by headnote or key number. Or you can filter by all of these restrictions at the same time.
- Review ample search results. Inexperienced researchers read only the first five or so case results and then move on. If you have taken the time to craft a useful and well-filtered search, take the time to look through at least twenty results — even if it means clicking through two pages.

II. Terms-and-Connectors Searching

Researchers usually use terms-and-connectors searches late in the case-finding process. These searches are usually appropriate after you have found your main cases but still need to fill gaps in the case law. Beginning the research process with terms-and-connectors searching, especially in an unfamiliar area of the law, may be frustrating: you will lack sufficient context to assess the number and quality of case results produced by your search.

Terms-and-connectors searching, also known as Boolean searching, requires more precision than natural-language searching. In natural-language searching, using any terms, in any order, with or without quotation marks, even with spelling mistakes, will always produce results. Some of the results may even be relevant. By contrast, terms-and-connectors searching is more finicky, but can also be more rewarding. It will only generate results that meet the specific criteria of your request. Sometimes, when no cases meet your criteria, you will get zero results. Sometimes you will get hundreds. For example, to search only for cases that contain the word "warranty" within ten words of the word "habitability," you would type in this: *warranty /10 habitability*. You may also want to restrict your results by jurisdiction (court and geography) and by type of document (only cases, in this instance). And here especially, if you have taken the time to craft a thoughtful search, make sure to read through the first few pages of results.

Because terms-and-connectors searching requires a high degree of precision, it is most effectively deployed once you already understand the law and have your main cases. But it can be a powerful research tool when utilized at the appropriate time. Continuing the example above, assume you represent a defendant landlord who is being sued for breaching the warranty of habitability. You have found many cases on point, but they have all held that the landlord *is* liable for breaching the warranty of habitability. Using terms-and-connectors, you could run a targeted search looking specifically for cases that contain the word "not" within the same sentence as "liable" (or breach) within the same sentence as "warranty of habitability." This search would help you locate only those cases where the defendant was found not liable, and thus help you fill the gap in your case law research.

Chapter 2 provides additional terms-and-connectors guidance, including in Table 2-4 a list of symbols and characters recognized by Lexis and Westlaw in terms-and-connectors searching.

III. Digests

Digests are subject indexes for case law. Digests are important for researchers to understand because they inform the way cases are categorized as routes to online research. This part of the chapter concentrates on digests published by West because West's key number system was one of the first and remains one of the most robust digests, but Lexis has a comparable research tool that is discussed at the end of the chapter.

This is how digests work: As every case is published, a West editor prepares a headnote for each point of law decided in that case. The headnote is categorized by broad topic (e.g., Landlord and Tenant) and specific idea (e.g., warranty of habitability). Those headnotes appear at the beginning of the case on Westlaw and in West's print reporters. The headnotes are also compiled in online databases and in print volumes, organized by the topic and the specific idea, which West calls a "key number." Online, cases involving a landlord-tenant dispute about the warranty of habitability are indexed together under the key number 233K1052. The number 233 represents the large topic Landlord and Tenant, while the second number represents warranty of habitability.

One reason digest key numbers are powerful research tools is that the collected headnotes of all the cases are organized by topic and key number order for each state. The key number 233K1052 will find cases on this topic in California, in Florida, and in the federal system. So headnotes are useful not only because they present short summaries of law at the top of each Westlaw case. Headnotes also serve a second important function: they are tools to organize the case into the appropriate digest under the assigned topic and key number. In an online digest, each headnote is linked to the case.

If you begin a research project with a good case already in hand, or as soon as you find a good case through other research approaches, the digest is an effective research tool. When you read the case on Westlaw, you will see that each headnote's topic and key number are hyperlinked to the online digest. Clicking on that hyperlink will bring up a list of cases with the same topic and key number. Thus you have a great entrance point to do further research using the digest.

You can also use a digest earlier in the process. The "Key Numbers" link on Westlaw's home page (and the list in the front of West digest volumes) provides an alphabetical list of all West topics — over 400 in all, ranging from the topic Abandoned and Lost Property to the topic Zoning and Planning. You could search all headnote titles by entering, for example, *habitability* in the "Title Search" box at the bottom of the page. Or you could open Landlord and Tenant and successive levels of that topic's outline until you arrive at key number 1052, which is warranty of habitability. Simply skimming the headings of a relevant topic could give you a quick overview of an area of law.

Lexis also allows you to research using its digest. When reading a case on Lexis, look for a series of subject headings just above the numbered headnotes, connected by > symbols. You will find a link to cases that address the same topic by clicking on the "Get documents" link from the drop-down menu.

Finally, digests are relevant even when doing natural-language searches. Because the headnote summaries are included in the research algorithm, your natural-language search results automatically take advantage of all the propriety content written by West or Lexis editors. So even if you are not doing digest research per se, you are benefitting from its content.

IV. Beyond Lexis and Westlaw

While Westlaw and Lexis still dominate the paid subscription service world, the market does have some competition, and more players are continually entering the field.

A. Bloomberg Law

Bloomberg Law, introduced in 2009, publishes cases from all jurisdictions in the United States and also offers editorial content. For instance, Bloomberg provides a system comparable to headnotes, called "Points of Law," which highlights holdings throughout legal opinions rather than at the beginning of cases. Generally speaking, Bloomberg is stronger in corporate and securities research than in case law research. For instance, it does not have a digest system or a fully developed citator service that informs readers whether a case is still good law.

B. Low-Cost Sources for Researching Judicial Opinions

Casemaker and Fastcase are two new low-cost legal research services. Both these services provide case law (and statute) searching as well as limited secondary sources. As of 2019, California is one of the three state bar associations that does not provide its members with a subscription to either Casemaker or Fastcase. However, some California county bar associations offer their members free Fastcase access, as does the California Lawyers Association.

Finally, Casetext is a low-cost legal research platform that includes access to federal cases and some state cases. This basic package is free, but for a subscription fee, attorneys can upload a brief and then use Casetext's artificial intelligence to generate research results relevant to the brief's content. As of 2019, more than 300 law firms had subscribed to Casetext.

C. Free Sources for Case Law

Cases are readily available for free on most courts' websites. Sometimes these sites do not allow searching by topic or search term, so you can look only for specific cases whose titles or docket numbers you already know.

The website for the California courts, courts.ca.gov, includes a fully searchable, free database. The site allows you to search by natural-language search terms, by citation, by party name, and by judge. An advanced search feature allows you to use a terms-and-connectors search. The site provides the official reporter version of the cases but does not include any editorial enhancements such as headnotes or case summaries.

Another free service is Google Scholar, found at scholar.google.com. On the home page, click on "Case law" below the search box and then choose between cases from federal courts or California courts; click on the link for "Select courts" to select courts from other jurisdictions. At that point, simply enter your search terms in the search box. Cases that come up in a Google Scholar search contain the full text of the case but do not include any of the editorial enhancements provided by Lexis or Westlaw. Running the same search without picking a court will bring up not only cases, but also secondary documents that relate to the search.

Other useful case-finding sites in the free legal research universe are FindLaw and the Cornell Legal Information Institute.

Appendix 4-A. Headnotes on Westlaw Edge

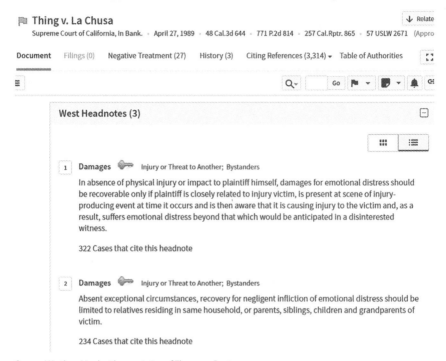

🏳 **Thing v. La Chusa**   ↓ Relate
   Supreme Court of California, In Bank. · April 27, 1989 · 48 Cal.3d 644 · 771 P.2d 814 · 257 Cal.Rptr. 865 · 57 USLW 2671 (Appro

Document   Filings (0)   Negative Treatment (27)   History (3)   Citing References (3,314) ▾   Table of Authorities   ⌗

≡   Q▾ ⬚ Go ⚑ ▾ ▣ ▾ 🔔 G

West Headnotes (3)   ⊟

                                                                              ⠿   ☰

1   **Damages** 🔑 Injury or Threat to Another; Bystanders

In absence of physical injury or impact to plaintiff himself, damages for emotional distress should
be recoverable only if plaintiff is closely related to injury victim, is present at scene of injury-
producing event at time it occurs and is then aware that it is causing injury to the victim and, as a
result, suffers emotional distress beyond that which would be anticipated in a disinterested
witness.

322 Cases that cite this headnote

2   **Damages** 🔑 Injury or Threat to Another; Bystanders

Absent exceptional circumstances, recovery for negligent infliction of emotional distress should be
limited to relatives residing in same household, or parents, siblings, children and grandparents of
victim.

234 Cases that cite this headnote

Source: Westlaw. Used with permission of Thomson Reuters.

Appendix 4-B. Headnotes on Lexis Advance®

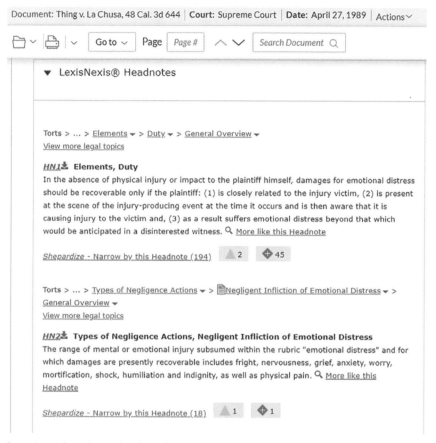

Source: Lexis Advance® screenshot. Copyright LexisNexis 2019, a division of RELX. All rights reserved. Lexis Advance is a registered trademark of Reed Elsevier, Inc. and is used with permission of LexisNexis.

Chapter 5

Constitutions

The California Constitution is the foundational governing document of the state. California has had two constitutions. The first constitution was ratified in 1849, nearly a year before California became a state. The second, and still operative, version of the constitution is referred to as the Constitution of 1879.

The provisions of the current California Constitution parallel many of the provisions of the United States Constitution, although the California Constitution provides for greater rights in some areas, such as education and privacy. Article I, section 1 lists the inalienable rights of California's citizens. Among those rights are "enjoying and defending life and liberty, acquiring, possessing, and protecting property, and pursuing and obtaining safety, happiness, and privacy."[1]

California has one of the longest constitutions in the United States because it covers not only fundamental rights typically associated with constitutional law but also issues often addressed in statutes. See Table 5-1. For example, Article I, section 2 provides the news media with a shield against an adjudication of contempt by a judicial, legislative, or administrative body for refusing to disclose sources or unpublished information. Because of the breadth of issues covered by the California Constitution, it is always wise to consider whether a constitutional provision affects a particular research problem.

I. Researching the California Constitution

The California Constitution is available on commercial and free online services as well as in hard copy volumes containing California statutes. In part because of this historical publication of constitutions with statutes, many online services include the constitution in statutory databases.

---

1. Cal. Const. art. I, § 1.

Table 5-1. Articles of the Constitution of California

Article I	Declaration of Rights
Article II	Voting, Initiative and Referendum, and Recall
Article III	State of California
Article IV	Legislative
Article V	Executive
Article VI	Judicial
Article VII	Public Officers and Employees
Article IX	Education
Article X	Water
Article XA	Water Resources Development
Article XB	Marine Resources Protection Act of 1990
Article XI	Local Government
Article XII	Public Utilities
Article XIII	Taxation
Article XIIIA	[Tax Limitation]
Article XIIIB	Government Spending Limitation
Article XIIIC	[Voter Approval for Local Tax Levies]
Article XIIID	[Assessment and Property Related Fee Reform]
Article XIV	Labor Relations
Article XV	Usury
Article XVI	Public Finance
Article XVIII	Amending and Revising the Constitution
Article XIX	Motor Vehicle Revenues
Article XIXA	Loans from the Public Transportation Account or Local Transportation Funds
Article XIXB	Motor Vehicle Fuel Sales Tax Revenues and Transportation Improvement Funding
Article XIXC	[Determination of Unlawful Taking or Diversion of Revenues from Specified Funds]
Article XIXD	Vehicle License Fee Revenues for Transportation Purposes
Article XX	Miscellaneous Subjects
Article XXI	Reapportionment of Senate, Assembly, Congressional and Board of Equalization Districts
Article XXII	[Architectural and Engineering Services]
Article XXXIV	Public Housing Project Law
Article XXXV	Medical Research

Note: Repealed and rejected articles are not listed.

Online, you can research the California Constitution using either Westlaw or Lexis. From the main Westlaw search page, find the California Constitution by clicking on "State Materials," then "California," then "California Statutes and Court Rules." The constitution is the first link within the statutory offerings. Alternatively, if you begin typing *California Constitution* in the universal search bar, Westlaw will suggest (1) a table of contents for a database containing the constitution, (2) a template for finding particular constitutional provisions, and (3) a list of databases that includes the California Constitution.

For Lexis, from the main "Explore Content" page, click on "State," then "California," then "CA-California Constitution." Another approach is to type *California Constitution* into the search bar on the Lexis home page. The result will be *Deering's California Code Annotated*, where you can enter search terms or select an article from a drop-down list.

The California Constitution is also available online without charge at leginfo. legislature.ca.gov/faces/codes.xhtml (click on "California Constitution" at the top of the list).[2] The website contains links to a table of contents and a search engine that allows searching by keyword. The site provides the constitutional text only, without any editorial enhancements.

Using print sources, you can locate the California Constitution in either of the hard copy California codes, *West's Annotated California Codes* or *Deering's California Codes Annotated*. The constitution appears in the first several volumes of both annotated codes. The index to the constitution appears in both code versions in the volume that contains the last section of the constitution. The print resources also include the text of the Constitution of 1849, the U.S. Constitution, and various federal statutes affecting California. The two publishers have not included exactly the same additional documents, so if possible check materials from both publishers when looking for a specific document.

Whether you are working online or in print, the research process is similar. As explained in Chapters 1 and 2, begin your research by generating a list of research terms from the facts and issues of your problem. Use those terms in either a keyword search or in an index and then record the references given. For example, using the term "Searches and Seizures" leads to references to Article I, sections 13 and 24 of the California Constitution.

To find cases and other authorities that have discussed a certain provision of the state constitution, look for the editorial material that follows the text

---

2. Information about the Constitution of 1849 is available on the State Archives website at sos.ca.gov/archives/collections/constitutions/.

Figure 5-1. Excerpt of Annotations for California Constitution

Art. I, Section 13	◄——————— Caption for Article I, section 13

Notes of Decisions

I. IN GENERAL 1–40	◄——————— Outline for
II. ISSUANCE OF WARRANT 41–130	annotations
III. SEARCHES AND SEIZURES 131–460	relevant to this
IV. ADMISSIBILITY OF EVIDENCE 461–520	constitutional
V. PRACTICE AND PROCEDURE 521–590	provision

271. Garage, expectation of privacy, searches and seizures	◄— Annotation to
A garage that is attached or adjacent to a home may give rise to a legitimate expectation of privacy therein. People v. Gomez (App. 3 Dist. 2005) 30 Cal.Rptr.3d 662, 130 Cal.App.4th 1008, rehearing denied, review denied.	a case from the California Court of Appeal

Source: *West's Annotated California Codes*, volume 1A Pt. 2, pp. 159, 365 (2016). Westlaw. Used with permission of Thomson Reuters..

of the particular section of each relevant article. This material includes historical notes, cross-references to statutes, citations to relevant law review articles, references to other materials published by the same publisher, references to analogous sections of the U.S. Constitution, and case annotations. These case annotations, called "Notes of Decisions," reference cases and attorney general opinions. Each annotation contains a brief summary of the source referenced and its citation, which will enable you to locate the actual source. See Figure 5-1. Be sure not to rely on the short summary; reading the text of the source itself is the only way to analyze its relevance to your research.

The Notes of Decisions are divided into subject-matter categories chosen by the publisher. In Lexis, Westlaw, and *West's Annotated California Codes*, these categories are outlined at the beginning of the Notes of Decisions; there is no similar outline in *Deering's California Codes Annotated*. If the version you are using has an outline, begin research in the annotations by looking over the outline for the area that is most pertinent to your research. This initial scanning of the outline is particularly important for researching sections of the constitution that have been discussed in many cases and attorney general opinions, such as in the example in Figure 5-1. Note that the annotations listed in these sources do not represent every authority that may be relevant to your research. To find additional cases on point, use the strategies discussed in Chapter 4. Chapter 10 explains using secondary sources as research tools.

II. Interpreting the California Constitution

California courts interpret a constitutional provision by considering the intent of those who enacted it. "To determine that intent, courts look first to the language of the constitutional text, giving the words their ordinary meaning."[3] In determining the "ordinary meaning" of the words, California courts may look to dictionaries, including legal dictionaries, and to decisions of other courts considering the same or similar language.[4] However, the words of the constitutional provision "must receive a liberal, practical common sense construction."[5] Moreover, the "literal language of enactments may be disregarded to avoid absurd results and to fulfill the apparent intent of the framers."[6]

When the language of the provision is not clear, California courts look to the source of the constitutional provision in interpreting its meaning. For provisions of the Constitution of 1879 that are still in effect, the court can look to the proceedings of the constitutional convention of 1879, as well as to the daily journal of the debates. Both are difficult to find in most libraries, although microfiche copies are available through the Congressional Information Services (CIS) *State Constitutional Conventions* set, which some libraries have.

Because the current California Constitution has been amended repeatedly, your research is likely to involve a section that was not part of the Constitution of 1879. The constitution may be *revised* through a constitutional convention called by the legislature.[7] It may be *amended* either through a proposal passed by a two-thirds vote of each house of the legislature[8] or by a voter initiative;[9] in either case, voters then have the opportunity to approve or reject the proposal or initiative.[10] The distinction between revision and amendment relates to the scope of the proposed change, and it can be crucial to the viability of the attempted change. The California Supreme Court has held that revision, which is a more sweeping constitutional change than amendment, must be done

---

3. *Leone v. Med. Bd. of Cal.*, 22 Cal. 4th 660, 665 (2000).

4. *Id.* at 666.

5. *L.A. Metro. Transit Auth. v. Pub. Util. Comm'n*, 59 Cal. 2d 863, 869 (1963) (quoting *Cty. of Alameda v. Sweeney*, 151 Cal. App. 3d 505, 512–13 (1957)).

6. *Amador Valley Joint Union High Sch. Dist. v. State Bd. of Equalization*, 22 Cal. 3d 208, 245 (1978).

7. Cal. Const. art. XVIII, § 2. California has not had a constitutional convention since 1879.

8. Cal. Const. art. XVIII, § 1.

9. Cal. Const. art. XVIII, § 3.

10. Cal. Const. art. XVIII, § 4.

through a constitutional convention and may not be accomplished through the initiative process.[11]

The court clarified the distinction between a revision and an amendment to the constitution in deciding a 2009 challenge to Proposition 8, the state ballot measure seeking to make same-sex marriage illegal.[12] The court identified a revision as one that works a "fundamental change in the *basic governmental plan or framework* established by the preexisting provisions of the California Constitution."[13] To be fundamental, a change must affect the structure of the state government "or the foundational powers of its branches."[14] The court has only once in recent decades found such a fundamental change in a voter-approved initiative.[15] In that case, the initiative purported to order the court itself not to find greater protections for criminal defendants under the California Constitution than they could receive under the U.S. Constitution.[16] The court held the initiative was a revision because it would limit the court's own powers and thus fundamentally change the judicial branch.

The initiative process was adopted in a number of states during the Progressive Era in the early 20th century in response to legislative corruption. California adopted it in 1911, largely to address the control of the legislature by the railroad companies. This process allows voters to propose amendments to the state constitution by placing measures on the election ballot. Voters begin the process by submitting a petition with a minimum number of signatures of qualified voters; this number is equal to 8% of the number of voters in the previous gubernatorial election (it is 5% for an initiative that proposes a statute).[17]

Because the initiative process has become increasingly popular since the success of the property tax initiative Proposition 13 in 1976, a ballot may contain more than one initiative that addresses the same subject. If the voters pass

---

11. *McFadden v. Jordan*, 32 Cal. 2d 330, 332–33 (1948).

12. *Strauss v. Horton*, 46 Cal. 4th 364, 441 (2009).

13. *Id.*

14. *Id.* (quoting *Legislature v. Eu*, 54 Cal. 3d 492, 509 (1991)).

15. *Raven v. Deukmejian*, 52 Cal. 3d 336, 356 (1990).

16. *Id.* at 350.

17. Cal. Const. art. II, §8(b). The lower percentage for statutes was approved by the voters in 1966 as an effort to encourage statutes rather than constitutional amendments. Joseph R. Grodin, Calvin R. Massey & Richard B. Cunningham, *The California State Constitution: A Reference Guide* 69–70 (1993).

two or more conflicting initiatives in the same election, the constitution includes the unusual rule that the measure that received the highest number of votes in the election prevails.[18]

If a court must look behind the wording of a section of the constitution added or amended by voter initiative, it looks for evidence of the voters' intent in the ballot summary and the arguments and analysis presented in the California *Voter Information Guide.* That pamphlet is prepared before each election and distributed to all registered voters by the secretary of state. Complete sets of these pamphlets from 1911 forward may be found in a few larger libraries, but most law libraries are likely to have voter pamphlets from only the last decade or two. The California Secretary of State's Office maintains an online database of voter pamphlets dating back to March 1996 at sos.ca.gov; click on "Election Data" under "Elections" and then "Voter Information Guides." From that site, you can access a searchable database of California ballot measures dating back to 1911, maintained by the University of California, Hastings College of the Law, by clicking on a link at the bottom of the page. The Hastings site permits a word search to find specific voter pamphlets.

III. Locating the United States Constitution

The federal constitution is the foundational law of the United States. It is available online on Lexis and Westlaw and at a variety of state and federal websites. You can also find the text of the Constitution or commentary on developments in constitutional law at the sites listed below:

- loc.gov/law/guide, a site maintained by the Law Library of Congress with links to a wide range of sites that include the text of the U.S. Constitution, as well as commentaries and annotations, some of which also provide search engines;
- findlaw.com/casecode/constitution, a free research site with a search engine; and
- scotusblog.com, a law blog written by lawyers, law professors, and law students that covers cases before the U.S. Supreme Court from certiorari through decision and live blogs during some oral arguments and when the Court announces opinions.

---

18. Cal. Const. art. II, § 10.

The federal constitution is available in hard copy along with the California Constitution in both *Deering's California Codes Annotated* and *West's Annotated California Codes*. It is also available in print in the first several volumes of *United States Code Annotated* and *United States Code Service*. These series are explained in Chapter 6.

Chapter 6

Statutes

In the hierarchy of legal authority in the United States, statutes come just below constitutions and ahead of cases and regulations as controlling sources of law. Therefore, for almost any research problem, you should check early on to see if there is a statute that affects your client's rights or responsibilities. Statutes create new rights or responsibilities when the legislature decides that the law needs to address a new issue, such as discrimination on the basis of sexual orientation or social media use by public employees. The legislature has also taken many common law rights and duties and enacted them into statutory law. For example, criminal law has been made almost completely statutory, sometimes by enacting the common law elements, sometimes by changing the elements, and sometimes by creating new crimes, such as stalking.[1] Even if you are researching a common law topic, a statute may be relevant to determine the statute of limitations, so you know how long you have to bring a claim.

This chapter discusses California state statutes: how they are organized, how to read them, how to conduct statutory research, and how to find cases interpreting statutes. The end of the chapter briefly addresses statutory interpretation, federal statutes, and court rules.

---

1. Section 646.9 of the California Penal Code defines and criminalizes stalking. It was added to the Penal Code in 1990.

Note that California is unusual in having both a subject name and a section number; only New York and Texas follow this pattern. Most states number their statutes using some combination of numerals and decimal points. For example, the following statutes define arson: Ariz. Rev. Stat. Ann. § 13-1701 (Arizona); Nev. Rev. Stat. § 205.005 (Nevada); Or. Rev. Stat. § 164.305 (Oregon); and Wash. Rev. Code § 9A.48.010 (Washington).

Table 6-1. California Statutory Codes

Business and Professions	Insurance
Civil	Labor
Civil Procedure	Military and Veterans
Commercial	Penal
Corporations	Probate
Education	Public Contract
Elections	Public Resources
Evidence	Public Utilities
Family	Revenue and Taxation
Financial	Streets and Highways
Fish and Game	Unemployment Insurance
Food and Agriculture	Vehicle
Government	Water
Harbors and Navigation	Welfare and Institutions
Health and Safety	

I. Structure of the California Code

California statutes can be enacted by either the legislature or the voters through the referendum and initiative process, which is similar to the initiative process for constitutional amendments, discussed in Chapter 5. Enacted statutes are then *codified*, meaning that they are grouped according to subject matter.[2] As each new statute is enacted, it is placed within the appropriate subject-matter code.

California statutes are grouped into twenty-nine individual subject-matter codes, which are listed in Table 6-1. Each of these codes is further divided into sections. For example, California Penal Code § 451 states the elements of arson. The citation to this statute is Cal. Penal Code § 451. California lawyers refer to California Penal Code § 451 as both a "statute" and a "code section."

Within various codes, sections may be grouped according to subtopics, though not all the codes use the same divisions. To continue the arson example, in the Penal Code, Title 13 addresses crimes against property, Chapter 1 concerns the crime of arson, and section 451 states what constitutes arson. Subdivisions of a section are indicated by (a), (b), (c), etc. Subdivision (a) of § 451

---

2. A few statutes and some initiative acts are never codified.

Figure 6-1. Example California Code Section

---

§ 451. Arson of structure, forest land or property; great bodily injury; inhabited structure or property; owned property; punishment.

A person is guilty of arson when he or she willfully and maliciously sets fire to or burns or causes to be burned or who aids, counsels, or procures the burning of, any structure, forest land, or property.

(a) Arson that causes great bodily injury is a felony punishable by imprisonment in the state prison for five, seven, or nine years.

(b) Arson that causes an inhabited structure or inhabited property to burn is a felony punishable by imprisonment in the state prison for three, five, or eight years.

(c) Arson of a structure or forest land is a felony punishable by imprisonment in the state prison for two, four, or six years.

Source: California Penal Code § 451.

provides punishment of up to nine years in prison for arson that causes great bodily injury. The citation to this subdivision is Cal. Penal Code § 451(a). Older statutes may include a letter without parentheses, such as § 403a, which should not be confused with subdivision (a) of a different § 403, which is written as § 403(a).

II. Reading Statutes

Statutes are the product of legislative compromise, so their language is often not clear enough to convey all possible meanings in one reading. Therefore, careful research may require multiple readings of the statutory language before you can fully understand its meaning and legal relevance.

It may also be necessary to read multiple code sections. The first section you read may list the elements of the claim you are researching. But the preceding statutory section may define a critical term used in an element, and the following statutory section may provide a defense to the claim. To illustrate, the code section in Figure 6-1 defines the crime of arson and indicates the possible punishments, depending on what kind of property was burned and whether anyone was injured. However, to know if your client acted "maliciously," you would have to look at section 450 of the Penal Code, which defines that term.

To ensure that you understand the statute, break it into its elements. Use bullet points or an outline to identify individual elements. Connecting words and punctuation may help delineate the relationships between the various el-

Table 6-2. Elements of Arson

- a person is guilty of arson who
  - willfully <u>and</u> maliciously
- acts by
  - setting fire to
  - burning
  - causing to be burned <u>or</u>
  - aiding, counseling, or procuring the burning of
- any
  - structure
  - forest land <u>or</u>
  - property

---

ements. For example, "and" means that all the elements must be present for the statute to apply, while "or" means that only one of the elements connected by "or" needs to be present. Table 6-2 breaks the first part of California Penal Code § 451 into its elements.

III. Statutory Research Process

You can access the California code in its unannotated form—that is, only the statutory language—online for free. In the simplest instance of statutory research, when you already know the citation for the statute you need, the unannotated code may suffice. The State of California provides a searchable database for statutes at leginfo.legislature.ca.gov/faces/codes.xhtml. You can do either a "Code Search" or a "Text Search." To find the relevant statute, it is best, however, to know the name of the code you want to search. The California code is also available for free, and searchable, at FindLaw.com/california-law.html.

In most research situations, however, you will have to determine which code sections are relevant, read the text of those statutes, and then read cases interpreting the statutes. Legislatures write statutes to apply to a wide variety of factual situations, so they are intentionally broad and can be ambiguous. Cases interpreting the statute may show how those ambiguous terms have been defined by the courts, and thus, how they apply to your client's specific facts.

Because you will typically want to find not only the statutory language but also cases interpreting that language, it will usually be necessary to review an annotated version of the California code. California has two different annotated codes: *Deering's California Codes Annotated*, published by Lexis, and *West's*

Annotated California Codes, published by West. They are available on Lexis and Westlaw, respectively, and are also bound into print volumes. The statutory language is identical in the Lexis and West versions of the annotated code, but the annotations are different.

The annotations within the California annotated code are valuable research tools whether you use them online or in print. The annotated codes reproduce the statutory text, but also provide the statute's history, cite law review articles and other secondary sources, and cite administrative materials related to the statute.

Perhaps most importantly, the annotated codes provide summaries of cases interpreting the statute, called Notes of Decisions. In *West's*, the annotations are the same case annotations used in the headnotes of cases in West reporters and in West digests (discussed in Chapters 3 and 4). The annotations in *Deering's* are written by its publisher, Lexis, so their wording differs from the wording in the annotations written by West. However, the concept is the same in both instances: the case summaries connect the researcher from the statute directly to the cases interpreting the statute in one research step.

These annotations are divided topically. For instance, in addition to looking at the subdivision of the arson statute that defines "maliciously," you can also find annotations to cases that interpret that term. You can also find cases that interpret terms not defined in the statute, such as "burning."

These valuable annotations, including the Notes of Decisions, are available only in the online annotated code (via paid subscription to Westlaw or Lexis) or the print *West's* or *Deering's* annotated code.

A. Researching the Annotated Code Online

The process for researching a statute varies depending on whether or not you are beginning with a citation to the statute. Below is a summary of both approaches.

1. Beginning with a Statutory Citation

On either Westlaw or Lexis, choose "California" as the jurisdiction and then type the citation into the main search box. You do not need the section symbol (§); rather, to find the arson statute discussed above, simply type *Cal Penal Code 451* or *California Penal Code 451*.

Once you have the relevant statutory section, both systems allow you to move to adjacent sections so you can navigate through the entire statute. On Westlaw, look toward the top of the page for a section symbol (§) with blue arrows on either side. You can also click on the "Table of Contents" tab to the left of the section symbol and blue arrows to get a pop-up window with the Table of Contents for the code. To navigate between adjacent sections on Lexis, click on the "Previous" or "Next" arrows at the top left and right corners of the screen. The link to the code's Table of Contents on Lexis is currently on the far left-hand side of the screen.

2. Beginning without a Statutory Citation

If you do not have a citation to the statute, online statutory research needs to be strategic. The California codes are long, and many statutes share the same language. In addition, any time that an annotation quotes the language of a statute, an online search will pick up that language.[3] Finally, as noted above, statutes are often written using very general language, which means that the same general language may turn up in statutes addressing very different subject matters.

Therefore, the best way to research statutes online is typically not with word searches, but with the California Statutes Index. Index searching means you look for your research terms in the index, which then leads you to the relevant statutory citation. To do thorough research, you will likely need to look up a few different terms before you find your statute, so generate alternate research terms before you begin your index research.

To find the California Statutes Index in Westlaw, go to "State Materials," then "California," then "California Statutes and Court Rules." On the right-hand side of that page, under "Tools and Resources," click on "California Statutes Index." Or you can type *California Statutes Index* into the search bar to pull up the index. Once within the index, to find the statute for stalking, click on "S" and scroll down (or use "Control-F") to find the word "Stalking." The first link listed under Stalking is the stalking statute: Cal. Penal Code § 646.9. Similarly, for the arson statute, click on "A" and find the word "Arson." The first link again takes you to a helpful starting point: Cal. Penal Code § 450 et seq. (The notation "et seq." refers to the section listed and the sections that follow it.) If you do not find a relevant statute using your first research term, use a synonym or an alternate research term—e.g., theft instead of petty theft.

On Lexis, finding the Index to Deering's California Annotated Code online is also very simple. Type *California statute* or *California code* into the main

---

3. In addition to using the Index, another way to eliminate the problem of getting results based on the annotations is to start by searching the unannotated version of the code. You can do this on both Lexis and Westlaw by using advanced search features.

Table 6-3. Researching California Statutes Online Using Word Searches

Lexis	Westlaw
1. Choose "State" in the content box below "Explore Content."	1. Click on "State Materials" below the "Browse" heading.
2. Choose "California" in the jurisdiction box below the main search box.	2. Choose "California."
3. Choose "Deering's California Codes Annotated."	3. Click on "California Statutes and Court Rules."
4. Enter search terms in the search box or use the "Terms" boxes to construct a terms-and-connectors search.	4. Enter search terms in the search box.
5. Narrow the results by entering further terms-and-connector words in the "Search within results" box.	5. Narrow the results by applying filters in the left margin: search within results, effective date, or statute title.
6. Choose from among the resulting cites.	6. Choose from among the resulting cites.

search bar, and one of the options that appears is CA-Deering's California Annotated—Index. Here, too, if you open the "A" options, you will find a listing for Arson, and the first link leads you to Penal §§ 450 to 457.1.

As convenient as the Index feature is, word searching is also a necessary skill. If you need to use word searches to find a California statute, follow the steps outlined in Table 6-3.

Regardless of how you find the statute, once you locate the California statutory section using either Westlaw or Lexis, you will be connected to the valuable annotations discussed above. Read through the Notes of Decisions, focusing on the topics that sound most relevant to your legal issue.

B. Researching the Annotated Code in Print

Despite the availability of the online annotated code, some attorneys still choose to conduct initial statutory research using print codes. The print research process is somewhat analogous to the online research process.

If you begin your research knowing the statutory citation, then, as in online research, you can simply find the statute in the physical annotated code volumes on the shelf. The name of each code is printed on the spine of the volume or volumes which contain that code. For example, "Health and Safety" and "Penal" are listed on the spines of the books, and the codes are shelved in alphabetical

Table 6-4. Outline for Statutory Research in Print

---

1. Generate research terms and use the index of *West's* or *Deering's* to find references to relevant statutes.

2. Locate, read, and analyze the statutes in the main volumes. If there is a pocket part or paper supplement, check for recent changes in the language of the statute.

3. Refer to annotations following the statutory language to find citations to cases and other authorities that interpret, apply, or analyze the statute.

4. If the resource you are using has a pocket part or supplementary volume, check that for more recent annotations.

5. Read and analyze the relevant cases.

---

order. Simply find the appropriate code and then look at the section numbers listed on the spine of each volume for that code. Page through the relevant volume to find the statute's section number.

More often, you will begin research knowing only your legal issue and the client's facts. In that situation, follow the outline in Table 6-4.

1. Find the Statute Using the Index

As in online statutory research, the index is the most effective place to begin print statutory research. Look for your research terms in the General Index volumes shelved at the end of either *Deering's California Codes Annotated* or *West's Annotated California Codes*. Write down references to statutes, including both the title of the code and the section number. Sometimes a research term will be included in the index but will be followed by a cross-reference to another index term. Referring to that term may lead you to other relevant statutes. See Figure 6-2 for an example of an index section.

2. Read the Statutory Language and Relevant Annotations

Both *Deering's* and *West's* contain the text of each statute, arranged in numerical order. For each statutory citation you found in the General Index, select the volume that contains the code name and section number in the citation, and then find the statute itself. Here there is an additional step beyond the online research process. Westlaw and Lexis are updated regularly (even daily) because online content is inexpensive to update. But because the print volumes are not republished nearly as frequently, the publishers include a pocket part or paperbound supplement that includes new statutes enacted

entire legislative body.[14] These statements, too, may be documented in the legislative bill files at the State Archives. For more recent legislation, they may also be documented in audio or video recordings of committee hearings or floor sessions.

Finally, do not overlook the possibility that the legislative history of the statute you are researching has already been well documented in a published court opinion or law review article. For example, *McGeorge Law Review* has published the annual "Review of Selected California Legislation" since 1970. Continuing our example, if you consulted volume 33 of the *McGeorge Law Review*, you would find that the author of SB 255 intentionally left the "significant risk" language undefined to allow police officers greater latitude when deciding if the law has been violated.[15] Strategies for locating law review articles are discussed in Chapter 10, and strategies for locating relevant cases are discussed in Chapter 4.

With these final four sources — and with other documents beyond those mentioned here that reflect what transpired during the legislative process — it is important to consider whether the sources or documents are accepted by the courts "as constituting cognizable legislative history."[16] For example, California courts generally do not consider statements by a bill's author to the press regarding a bill's objectives indicative of legislative intent where "there is no reliable indication that the Legislature as a whole was aware of that objective and believed the language of the proposal would accomplish it."[17] So even if you locate documents containing such statements, a California court is unlikely to rely on those documents in construing a statute.

V. Initiative and Referendum in California[18]

Legislation in California can also come directly from the people through the initiative and referendum processes, discussed in Chapter 5 on the California

---

14. *See, e.g., In re Marriage of Siller*, 187 Cal. App. 3d 36, 46 (1986) (considering floor statement of sponsoring legislator).

15. Jaeson D. White, Student Author, *Sit Right Here Honey, I'll Be Right Back: The Unattended Child in Motor Vehicle Safety Act*, 33 McGeorge L. Rev. 343, 350 (2001–2002).

16. *Kaufman & Broad Communities, Inc.*, 133 Cal. App. 4th at 31–39 (identifying documents that are and are not considered "cognizable legislative history" in California's Third District Court of Appeal).

17. *People v. Garcia*, 28 Cal. 4th 1166, 1175 n.5 (2002).

18. This description of the initiative and referendum process is taken largely from the "Statewide Initiative Guide" found on the website of the California Secretary of State at elections.cdn.sos.ca.gov/ballot-measures/pdf/statewide-initiative-guide.pdf.

Constitution. Members of the public must follow four steps to put an initiative on the ballot.

- The first step is writing the initiative, which proponents can do themselves. They can also get help from the Legislative Counsel's office.
- The second step is to get a title and a summary of the chief purpose of the initiative from the attorney general. If the attorney general determines that the proposed legislation would have a fiscal impact, the Department of Finance and the Legislative Analyst prepare an analysis of that impact.
- The third step is the one that most California residents are familiar with: circulation of the initiative petition to collect voter signatures. The number of signatures for a statutory initiative must equal at least 5% of the total votes cast for governor in the most recent gubernatorial election. Signatures for a constitutional initiative must equal at least 8% of the total votes cast for governor in the last gubernatorial election. When an initiative's proponents have collected 25% of the signatures required to place the measure on the ballot, the measure is sent to the California Legislature. Each house assigns the measure to the appropriate committees, which hold joint public hearings. The legislature cannot amend the initiative or prevent it from appearing on the ballot, although an initiative's proponents may withdraw the measure.
- The final step is filing the signatures with the appropriate county elections official, who must then verify the signatures to assure that they represent the registered voters in that county. Initiatives must qualify at least 131 days before a statewide general election to appear on the ballot.

Voters may also approve or reject legislation adopted by the California Legislature through the referendum process. Although the system is similar to that used for initiatives, there are important timing differences. Referendum petitions must be circulated and filed within ninety days of enactment of the bill that is being referred and can qualify for the ballot up to thirty-one days before a statewide general election.

You can track initiatives and referenda as they progress from initial proposal to certification on the California Secretary of State's website at sos.ca.gov. Click on "Elections," then, under "Ballot Measures," click on "Initiative and Referendum Status."

For statutes enacted by initiative, when the text of the statute is unclear, courts consider the intent of the voters in interpreting the meaning of the statute. As explained in Chapter 5, courts look for evidence of the voters' intent in the ballot summary and the arguments and analysis presented to the voters in the California *Voter Information Guide*. Chapter 5 explains where to find these materials.

VI. Federal Legislative Research

Researching the federal legislative process involves roughly the same steps as researching California's laws, though some of the terminology is different. The United States Congress meets for two-year terms, beginning on January 3 of each odd-numbered year after a November general election. Each term is divided into two sessions, one for each year.

Bills are numbered sequentially in each chamber of Congress. Generally, Senate bill numbers are preceded by an "S," and House bill numbers are preceded by "H.R." for "House of Representatives." When a federal statute is enacted, it is printed as a *slip law* and assigned a *public law number*. This number is in the form Pub. L. No. 107-110, where the numerals before the hyphen represent the two-year Congressional term in which the statute was enacted and the numerals after the hyphen are assigned chronologically. The public law number given above is for the No Child Left Behind Act, which was passed in 2002 during the 107th Congress.

The new statute is later published as a *session law* in a series called *United States Statutes at Large*, which is the federal counterpart of *Statutes and Amendments to the Codes* in California. Session laws are designated by volume and page number in *Statutes at Large*, e.g., 115 Stat. 1425. Finally, the statute is assigned a *statutory citation* when it is codified with statutes having similar topics in the *United States Code*. The citation for the first section of the No Child Left Behind Act is 20 U.S.C. § 6301.

A. Federal Bill Tracking

Using online sources for bill tracking is often easier than using print sources and leads to more comprehensive results. The Library of Congress, congress.gov, provides bill summaries and status, committee reports, and the *Congressional Record* (which records debate in the House and Senate). The Government Publishing Office site, govinfo.gov, also contains bills, selected hearings and reports, and the *Congressional Record*. Coverage varies even within a single site, so check carefully. Both websites are updated daily.

B. Federal Legislative History

As with California legislative history, federal legislative history research begins with the statutory citation. If you do not know the citation, use an annotated code to find it (as described in Chapter 6). With a statutory citation, you can find the session law citation and public law number following the text of the statute, which will lead to the legislative history of the bill as it worked its way through Congress.

In conducting federal legislative history research, you are looking for sources that are often very different from the sources available for California legislative history research. Federal legislative history is found in committee reports, materials from committee hearings, and transcripts of floor debates, none of which exist in California. Congressional committee reports are often lengthy documents that contain the committee's analysis of the bill, the reasons for enacting it, and the views of any members who disagreed with those reasons. Congressional hearing materials include transcripts from the proceedings as well as documents such as prepared testimony and exhibits. These documents may be available in local federal depository libraries, but not all libraries are likely to have all reports and hearing materials. Finally, unlike the *Journal of the Senate* and the *Journal of the Assembly* in California, which print only records of votes without any transcripts of debates, the *Congressional Record* publishes transcripts of floor debates in the Senate and House of Representatives.

The sites noted earlier in this chapter for tracking federal legislation also provide useful information for legislative history research. The Library of Congress site at congress.gov provides bill summaries and status, committee reports, and the *Congressional Record*. The Government Publishing Office site at govinfo.gov contains bills, selected hearings and reports, and the *Congressional Record*. A popular site for researching federal legislative history is ProQuest Congressional.

Researchers have already compiled legislative histories for certain federal statutes that lawyers consider important. One reference book that identifies legislative histories of major federal statutes is *Sources of Compiled Legislative Histories*.[19] In addition, as is the case with California legislative history, there may be a published opinion or law review article that thoroughly reviews the legislative history of the statute you are researching.

---

19. Nancy P. Johnson, *Sources of Compiled Legislative Histories: A Bibliography of Government Documents, Periodical Articles, and Books* (Ronald E. Wheeler et al. eds., 4th ed. 2018).

Appendix 7-A. Final Bill History

This is the history of SB 255, which was enacted in 2001. The history is taken from the Office of Legislative Counsel website at leginfo.ca.gov/pub/ 01-02/bill/sen/sb_0251-0300/sb_255_bill_20011013_history.html.

COMPLETE BILL HISTORY

BILL NUMBER: S.B. No. 255

AUTHOR: Speier

TOPIC: Crimes: unattended children in vehicles.

TYPE OF BILL:	Inactive
	Non-Urgency
	Non-Appropriations
	Majority Vote Required
	State-Mandated Local Program
	Fiscal
	Non-Tax Levy

BILL HISTORY

2001

Oct. 13	Chaptered by Secretary of State. Chapter 855, Statutes of 2001.
Oct. 12	Approved by Governor.
Sept. 19	Enrolled. To Governor at 3 p.m.
Sept. 12	Senate concurs in Assembly amendments. (Ayes 24. Noes 11. Page 2815.) To enrollment.
Sept. 5	In Senate. To unfinished business.
Sept. 5	Read third time. Passed. (Ayes 53. Noes 17. Page 3456.) To Senate.
Aug. 31	Read second time. To third reading.
Aug. 30	From committee: Do pass as amended. (Ayes 13. Noes 3.) Read second time. Amended. To second reading.
Aug. 22	From committee with author's amendments. Read second time. Amended. Re-referred to committee.

July 16	Read second time. Amended. Re-referred to Com. on APPR.
July 14	From committee: Do pass as amended, but first amend, and re-refer to Com. on APPR. (Ayes 13. Noes 2.)
July 2	From committee with author's amendments. Read second time. Amended. Re-referred to committee.
June 25	To Com. on TRANS.
June 6	In Assembly. Read first time. Held at Desk.
June 6	Read third time. Passed. (Ayes 26. Noes 10. Page 1468.) To Assembly.
June 5	Read third time. Amended. To third reading.
May 25	Read second time. Amended. To third reading.
May 24	From committee: Do pass as amended. (Ayes 8. Noes 3. Page 1217.)
May 22	Set for hearing May 24.
May 16	Hearing postponed by committee.
May 15	Set for hearing May 21.
May 14	Set, first hearing. Hearing canceled at the request of author.
May 7	Set for hearing May 14.
May 3	From committee with author's amendments. Read second time. Amended. Re-referred to committee.
Apr. 30	Read second time. Amended. Re-referred to Com. on APPR.
Apr. 26	From committee: Do pass as amended, but first amend, and re-refer to Com. on APPR. (Ayes 5. Noes 0. Page 657.)
Apr. 5	From committee with author's amendments. Read second time. Amended. Re-referred to committee.
Mar. 12	Set, first hearing. Hearing canceled at the request of author. Set for hearing April 17.
Mar. 5	Set for hearing April 3.
Mar. 1	To Com. on PUB. S.

Feb. 16	From print. May be acted upon on or after March 18.
Feb. 15	Introduced. Read first time. To Com. on RLS. for assignment. To print.

Appendix 7-B. Bill Analysis

The following excerpt is taken from seven pages of analysis produced by the Assembly Committee on Transportation as it considered SB 255. Lengthy omissions are indicated by asterisks. The full committee analysis is available at leginfo.legislature.ca.gov/faces/billAnalysisClient.xhtml.

BILL ANALYSIS	SB 255
	Page A

ASSEMBLY COMMITTEE ON TRANSPORTATION
John Dutra, Chair
SB 255 (Speier) — As Amended: July 2, 2001

<u>SENATE VOTE</u>: 26–10

<u>SUBJECT</u>: Crimes: unattended children in vehicles

<u>SUMMARY</u>: Makes it an infraction to leave a child under the age of six unattended in a motor vehicle, as specified, and creates a fund for an educational campaign regarding the dangers of leaving a child in a vehicle. Specifically, <u>this bill</u>:

1) Creates the "Unattended Child in Motor Vehicle Safety Act" and contains intent language stating that it is the purpose of this division of the Vehicle Code to help prevent injuries to, and the death of, young children from the effects of being left alone in a motor vehicle, to help educate parents and caretakers about the dangers of leaving children alone in a motor vehicle, and to authorize a monetary fine to be imposed on a person for leaving a young child alone in a motor vehicle in circumstances that pose a life safety risk.

***

2) Provides that the "Unattended Child in Motor Vehicle Safety Act" shall be known and cited as "Kaitlyn's Law."

<u>EXISTING LAW</u> makes it a crime for any person, under circumstances or conditions likely to produce great bodily harm or death, to willfully cause or permit any child to suffer, or inflict thereon, unjustifiable physical pain or mental suffering, or having the care or custody of any child, to willfully cause or permit the person or health of that child to be injured, or willfully cause or permit that child to be placed in a situation where his or her person or health is endangered. This crime is punishable by imprisonment in a county jail not exceeding one year, or in the state prison for two, four, or six years. Existing law also provides that no person shall leave standing a locked vehicle in which

there is any person who cannot readily escape therefrom and that doing so constitutes an infraction.

FISCAL EFFECT: According to the Senate Appropriations Committee, the bill appears to redirect 60% of state penalties, county penalties and other penalties and assessments that otherwise would go according to statutory allocation for various purposes.

COMMENTS: This bill is premised on the belief that an educational campaign approach directed at social ills does not work unless it is coupled with an enforcement component.

***

Areas of Concern:

1) Most cases involving unattended children in vehicles occur on private property, such as parking lots and driveways. Law enforcement agencies might not have jurisdiction in such areas and, therefore, would be unable to cite for violation of this new law.

2) The first standard triggering the application of this new law (conditions that present a significant risk to the child's health and safety) is vague for lack of definition.

***

Analysis Prepared by: Joseph Furtado / TRANS. / (916) 319-2093

Chapter 8

Administrative Law

Administrative law is primary authority like constitutions, statutes, and cases. It differs from those primary authorities, however, because it issues from the executive branch. Administrative law includes both regulations and adjudicatory decisions of governmental agencies. This chapter introduces administrative law and the agencies that promulgate that law. In addition to explaining California administrative regulations, this chapter covers agency decisions and attorney general opinions, and it briefly introduces federal administrative law.

I. Administrative Law and Governmental Agencies

California defines state agencies to include "every state office, officer, department, division, bureau, board, and commission."[1] The online directory of state agencies lists over 500 state agencies, ranging from the Department of Alcoholic Beverage Control to the Workforce Investment Board.[2]

Agencies are created in three fundamental ways. First, many agencies are created by the legislature. While agencies are generally part of the executive branch, the source of their authority is often an *enabling statute* passed by the legislature. Second, some California agencies are created, or their creation is authorized, by the state constitution. For example, the constitution created the Public Utilities Commission.[3] Such agencies are designated "constitutional agencies," and the usual rules of administrative law do not apply to them.

---

1. Cal. Gov't Code § 11000 (Deering 2010).
2. The State Agencies Directory can be found at ca.gov/agenciesall/. Not all of the state agencies listed exercise all the functions discussed below. Although all of these bodies qualify as "state agencies," the California Code of Regulations (CCR) currently includes regulations from about 200 agencies. *See* govt.westlaw.com/calregs/Help.
3. *See* Cal. Const. art. XII.

Third, agencies may be created by voter initiative. For example, in 1984 a voter initiative amended the California Constitution to authorize the California State Lottery and enacted the California State Lottery Act of 1984.[4] That act created the Lottery Commission, the agency that operates the lottery.[5]

The statutory and constitutional provisions that create agencies establish the powers and duties of the agencies. Each agency must work within the limits set by its enabling statute or provision; all actions taken and regulations issued by an agency that exceed the powers granted in the enabling law are void.[6] Be sure to research the enabling statute or provision for all agencies, including those authorized by the California Constitution or a voter initiative.

Unlike other parts of the government, administrative agencies can perform all three governmental functions — legislative, executive, and judicial.

- Agencies exercise a legislative function when they promulgate regulations that interpret and apply statutes; these regulations are similar in form and have similar authority to statutes. In fact, California regulations are often referred to as "quasi-legislative rules."
- Agencies are part of the executive branch of the government, so they also exercise executive authority. Examples of this authority are licensing people to practice professions, such as architecture and cosmetology, and conducting investigations to see whether laws are being followed, such as anti-poaching operations by the Department of Fish and Game.
- Agencies also hold quasi-judicial hearings to apply the agency's rules in specific cases, such as the denial of government benefits. These hearings are similar to court proceedings, but are less formal.

In general, agencies function within the bounds of an Administrative Procedure Act (APA). California's APA can be found in the Government Code at sections 11340–11361. Some agencies and the actions of some agencies are exempt from the APA under section 11340.9 and sections 11351–11361, although many of these exemptions have their own exceptions. These exemptions and exceptions apply, for example, to California's Public Utilities Commission, Division of Workers' Compensation, and Lottery Commission.

---

4. *See* Cal. Const. art. IV, § 19, subd. (d); Cal. Gov't Code §§ 8880–8880.72 (Deering 2010 & Supp. 2017); *see also* California Ballot Pamphlet, 1984 General Election, at repository.uchastings.edu/cgi/viewcontent.cgi?article=1931&context=ca_ballot_props.

5. Cal. Gov't Code § 8880.15.

6. *Morris v. Williams*, 67 Cal. 2d 733, 748 (1967).

Each of the three branches of government has some oversight of agency actions. The legislative branch establishes agency powers and can add to them or remove them with subsequent legislation. The legislative branch also provides operating funds to agencies. The courts determine in contested cases whether regulations are authorized by their enabling statutes or provisions. The governor supervises all state agencies, and the executive branch exercises control over many agencies by appointing their highest officials.

II. Administrative Regulations

The California APA establishes not only the procedures for adopting, amending, and appealing agency regulations, but also the Office of Administrative Law (OAL) in the executive branch. The OAL ensures that citizens can understand regulations as written, that regulations are authorized by statute, and that they are consistent with other law. All proposed regulations must be approved by the OAL before they are filed with the secretary of state's office, and the OAL can disapprove proposed regulations.[7]

All regulations are subject to the APA's rulemaking procedures. A regulation is a "rule, regulation, order, or standard of general application or amendment, supplement, or revision of any rule, regulation, order, or standard adopted by any state agency to implement, interpret, or make specific the law enforced or administered by it, or to govern its procedure."[8] Or, as the OAL itself says, "if a rule looks like a regulation, reads like a regulation, and acts like a regulation, it will be treated by the courts as a regulation whether or not the issuing agency so labeled it."[9]

Agencies promulgate regulations to implement a statute, to interpret a statute, or to make a statute specific. Agencies are the "experts" in the field, so the legislature leaves to the agency the task of supplying the details that the legislature is unable to include in the more general statute. See Table 8-1. For example, regulations may provide guidance based on an agency's understanding of a relevant statute or determine the procedural deadlines and format for agency filings.

---

7. Agencies can appeal these disapprovals to the governor. A link to the governor's resulting decisions can be found on the OAL website at oal.ca.gov.

8. Cal. Gov't Code § 11342.600 (Deering 2010).

9. Office of Administrative Law, *What Is a Regulation?* 2 (Apr. 6, 2006) (available at oal.ca.gov/wp-content/uploads/sites/166/2017/05/What_Is_a_Regulation.pdf) (citing *St. Water Resources Control Bd. v. Off. of Admin. L.*, 12 Cal. App. 4th 697, 702 (1993)).

Table 8-1. Example of the Relationship between Statutes and Regulations

Statute: Because of the importance of agriculture to the California economy, the legislature enacted a law addressing "Certification, Processing and Canning, and Canned Foods." Under the terms of the statute, the Department of Food and Agriculture, an agency, was directed to establish standards for processing various agricultural products, including tomatoes.

Regulation: A regulation issued by the Department of Food and Agriculture specifies that "Any load of tomatoes which is offered for delivery to a canner shall be rejected and turned back to the grower if in excess of 2 percent, by weight, is affected by worm damage. A tomato is scoreable for worm damage when a worm has penetrated the flesh."

Sources: Cal. Food & Agric. Code § 40761(a) (Deering 1997); Cal. Code Regs. tit. 3, § 1332.1 (2013).

Once a regulation is promulgated, it is published in the California Code of Regulations (CCR), which is divided into titles. The titles are then subdivided in an outline format that may include divisions, chapters, subchapters, groups, subgroups, articles, and sections, although a division may use only some of these subdivisions. Regardless of the outline format chosen, the sections within a particular title are numbered consecutively from one to the highest number. For example, the regulation discussed in Table 8-1 can be found in Title 3 at § 1332.1. See Table 8-2 for a list of the CCR titles.

Although regulations and statutes are both primary authority, regulations are subordinate to statutes. In any conflict between a regulation and a statute, the statute has priority.

III. Researching California Administrative Regulations

The process for researching California administrative law is outlined in Table 8-3 and explained in detail on the next pages.

A. Underground Regulations

Given the expansive definition of a regulation cited above, it may seem impossible for an agency to believe any action with general applicability would not qualify as a "regulation." However, California agencies have routinely created policies or procedures that they believe do not have to be promulgated as regulations using the procedures established in the APA. These agency actions are referred to as "underground regulations," and they cannot be enforced legally.

Table 8-2. California Code of Regulations Titles

1. General Provisions	15. Crime Prevention and Corrections
2. Administration	16. Professional and Vocational
3. Food and Agriculture	17. Public Health
4. Business Regulations	18. Public Revenues
5. Education	19. Public Safety
6. Governor [no regulations filed]	20. Public Utilities and Energy
7. Harbors and Navigation	21. Public Works
8. Industrial Relations	22. Social Security
9. Rehabilitative and Developmental Service	23. Water
10. Investment	24. Building Standards*
11. Law	25. Housing and Community
12. Military and Veterans Affairs	26. Toxics
13. Motor Vehicles	27. Environmental Protection
14. Natural Resources	28. Managed Health Care

* Title 24 is now published by the California Building Standards Commission. The Commission republishes Title 24 in its entirety every three years. It is available in print, and some parts are available online at the Commission's website at dgs.ca.gov/BSC.

If you think an agency has taken an action against your client based on what you believe is an underground regulation, you can challenge the underground regulation by filing a petition with the OAL. If the OAL accepts your petition, it will issue an advisory opinion, referred to as a "determination." You can also ask a court to enjoin enforcement of an underground regulation.[10]

Table 8-3. Outline for California Administrative Law Research

1. Find the statutory or constitutional provision granting the agency power to act.
2. Research case law to determine whether the agency acted within that power.
3. Find the text of the relevant regulation in the California Code of Regulations (CCR).
4. Update the regulation in the *California Regulatory Notice Register* ("Z Register") to find any proposed changes.
5. Find agency and judicial decisions applying the regulation in similar circumstances.

10. Section 11350(a) of the APA authorizes any interested person to bring an action for a declaratory judgment to test the validity of a regulation.

B. Researching the Enabling Statute or Provision

Assuming you are dealing with a promulgated regulation, the initial question in analyzing the regulation is whether the agency that adopted it acted within its power. If that is in doubt, your first step in researching a regulation is to find the enabling statute or constitutional provision that gives the agency power to act. You may begin your research with a cite to the enabling law. If not, you can find the cite by starting with the regulation itself, a process explained below in section C. Look at the authority citation following the text of the regulation to identify the statute or constitutional provision that purports to give the agency the power to adopt the regulation.

Once you identify the enabling law, the next step is to find cases interpreting that statute or constitutional provision. This research will help determine whether the agency acted within the limits of its power in adopting the regulation. Chapters 5 and 6 explain the process of researching California statutes and constitutional provisions as well as annotations to relevant cases. Chapters 3 and 4 explain how to find additional cases using reporters and digests. If the agency's power is clear, skip this inquiry and move directly to finding and analyzing the relevant regulation, as explained next.

C. California Code of Regulations

The OAL is charged with publishing all California regulations in the CCR. The OAL has licensed publication of both online and print versions of the CCR to West. The OAL website provides a link to the online version of the CCR at ccr.oal.ca.gov, where you can click on a list of CCR titles and work your way through the table of contents for each title. The print version of the CCR is *Barclays Official California Code of Regulations* ("*Barclays*"), which is published in three-ring binders. *Barclays* includes the full text of all promulgated regulations. It is updated weekly through the *California Code of Regulations Supplement* (the "*CCR Supplement*"), which consists of insert pages for the *Barclays* binders.[11]

Another print source of information is *Barclays Digest of New Regulations*, which is published along with the weekly *CCR Supplement*. The *Digest* includes all amendments to regulations that the OAL has approved and filed

---

11. Each issue of the *CCR Supplement* is identified by *Register* year and weekly issue number, e.g., *Register* 2007, No. 30. The "Filing Instructions" for each issue of the *CCR Supplement* should be located in the Title 1 binder; check the date of the most recent *CCR Supplement* in your library's *Barclays* to find out how recent your pages are.

Figure 8-1. Example of a California Regulation

Title 19 Cal. Code Regs.

§ 986 Classification

(a) Fireworks or pyrotechnic devices that are to be used or sold for use in this state and found by the State Fire Marshal to come within the definition of "party poppers", "snap caps", "safe and sane", "agricultural and wildlife", "model rocket motors", "high power rocket motors", "emergency signaling device", or "exempt" fireworks shall be classified as such by the State Fire Marshal.

EXCEPTION: Special Effects items developed and compounded on location for single time usage.

(b) The classification of an item shall not be construed as conferring classification to any similar item without the approval of the State Fire Marshal. The trade name of an item shall not be changed without notifying the State Fire Marshal 30 days prior to such change.

NOTE: Authority cited: Sections 12552 and 12553, Health and Safety Code. Reference: Sections 12560–12569 and 12671, Health and Safety Code.

HISTORY

1. Renumbering of article heading, amendment of section text and new Note filed 4-14-92; operative 5-14-92 (Register 92, No. 21).

2. Amendment of subsection (a) filed 6-24-94; operative 6-24-94 (Register 94, No. 25).

Source: *Barclays Official California Code of Regulations*, volume 25, page 67 (2012).

with the secretary of state in a one-week period. The *Digest* is a useful source to check to determine if a regulation you are researching has been changed in the recent past.

Researching California regulations in print is relatively straightforward. *Barclays* includes a "Master Index," which is published in its own binder and is usually shelved at the end of the entire CCR series. The Master Index is divided into a subject index and a "Table of Statutes to Regulations." It is best to search in the subject index by topic rather than by agency name because entries for specific agencies lead primarily to regulations about the organization and procedures of that agency. The Master Index is issued on a semiannual basis.

Once you find a regulation, read the text of the regulation carefully. Many techniques used for reading statutes apply equally to reading regulations. For example, you should always look for a separate rule that provides definitions, be aware of cross-references, read the text several times, and outline any complicated provisions. Figure 8-1 provides an example of a California regulation concerning fireworks.

Following the text of each regulation is a "Note" that includes an authority citation to the statute that enables the agency to adopt regulations and a reference citation that indicates the statute(s) that this regulation implements, interprets, or makes specific. After these citations is a "History" section, which is provided whenever a regulation is adopted, amended, repealed, renumbered, or includes an editorial correction. Because the legal issue you are researching will be controlled by the regulation in effect when the issue arose, read the history note to learn of any changes to the rule since that time.[12]

D. *California Regulatory Notice Register*

Agencies take regulatory actions daily. To inform the public of these actions, the OAL publishes the *California Regulatory Notice Register* weekly. It is commonly referred to as the "Z Register."

The Z Register serves several functions. First, it is the location where agencies are required by the APA to publish all proposed actions on regulations. These notices may include an "informative digest/policy overview" discussing the nature of the proposed regulation, a prediction of the likely cost to local agencies, a consideration of reasonable alternatives, and the effect on small business. The notices must include information on where the public can get the full text of the proposed regulation, when and where members of the public may submit comments, and the time and place of any public hearing. Second, the Z Register contains notices of general public interest, OAL determinations on alleged underground regulations, OAL decisions disapproving proposed regulatory changes, and a summary of regulations filed with the secretary of state.

The Z Register is available on the OAL website and in print. Z Registers from 2002 to the present are available online on the OAL website. For Z Registers prior to 2002, contact the State Law Library in Sacramento.

Researching in the Z Register in print to find proposed regulatory action is difficult. There is no index or other finding tool for the Z Register. However, under the APA, agency action must be completed within one year of the date of the publication of the notice of proposed action. Therefore, a researcher

---

12. It may also be helpful to contact the agency that adopted the regulation and request the rulemaking file. The rulemaking file may reveal the legislative history of the regulation, including the legislative intent of the agency that adopted the regulation, any amendments to the proposed regulation as it moved through the APA process, and public comments on the proposed regulation as well as the agency's response to any comments received. As an alternative, a practicing attorney may rely on the commercial services discussed in Chapter 7 that compile legislative history for a fee.

needs to go through only twelve months of Z Registers following the first notice to determine what happened to the proposed regulation. The issues for the year in which you are researching and for some of the preceding year may be available in your library.

The Government Code requires that all agencies that intend to undertake regulatory activity in a calendar year must prepare a rulemaking calendar by January 30 of that year. The combined calendar for all agencies becomes available several months later.[13] You can use this calendar to learn what administrative actions are scheduled for the upcoming year, which will tell you if you need to keep track of notices in the Z Register that might affect regulations that you are researching.

The most reliable source of information on pending regulatory action is the agency itself. You can contact agencies directly. In addition, agencies often have their own websites. Any agency that has a website is required by the APA to post information concerning its regulatory actions on the site.[14] If you need to track pending regulations on a regular basis, members of the public and interested organizations can request that a state agency put them on a mailing list to be notified directly of any proposed regulatory actions.[15]

E. Agency Decisions

The APA not only controls administrative regulations and rulemaking, but also provides for agency adjudications.[16] Adjudications primarily involve decisions of those agencies that issue professional or occupational licenses and administer entitlement benefits; adjudications also concern personnel decisions of many agencies. Some adjudications occur through confidential mediation or arbitration. Other adjudications involve a hearing process presided over by an administrative law judge (ALJ); these decisions become public record. California law authorizes both informal and formal hearings. Some larger agencies have their own ALJs, but others use a centralized pool of independent ALJs provided by the Office of Administrative Hearings.

Agency decisions must be written, must be based on the record, and must include a statement of both the factual and the legal basis for the decision.[17]

---

13. The rulemaking calendar is available on the OAL website at oal.ca.gov. First click on "Publications" at the top of the screen, and then click on "Rulemaking Calendar."

14. Cal. Gov't Code § 11340.85(c) (Deering 2010).

15. Cal. Gov't Code § 11346.4(a)(1) (Deering 2010).

16. Cal. Gov't Code §§ 11370–11528 (Deering 2010 & Supp. 2013).

17. Cal. Gov't Code §§ 11425.10(a)(6), 11425.50 (Deering 2010).

Since 1997, adjudicative decisions by agencies may be designated as precedential; barring such a designation, an agency may not rely on a previous decision as precedent.[18] Agencies must keep an index of "significant legal and policy determinations made in precedent decisions," and the index must be available to the public by subscription.[19]

Despite the requirements that adjudicatory decisions must be written and that agencies must keep an index of precedential decisions, finding such decisions is difficult. No method of printing, indexing, or digesting has been created. Some decisions can be found on either Lexis or Westlaw. Agencies that have websites and issue decisions include precedential decisions and perhaps non-precedential decisions on their websites. But this means you have to know which agency's website to search and may have to look around the website carefully to find the decisions. Agencies will respond to direct requests, but you will generally need both a case name and a case number to get a useful answer.

Administrative orders may be appealed to a California Superior Court for review. California courts have jurisdiction to review the validity of both regulations and agency adjudications.[20] Researching case law may reveal cases that address the agency rules and orders relevant to your research.

F. Attorney General Opinions

As the state's lawyer, the attorney general provides opinions that are similar to the advice of an attorney to a client. A formal opinion from the attorney general responds to a specific question posed by a state or local public officer. The California Constitution and statutes restrict those who can ask for a formal opinion from the attorney general to constitutional officers, legislators, state agencies, state boards or commissions, district attorneys, county counsels, sheriffs, city prosecutors, and judges.

Even though attorney general opinions come from a branch of the government, they are not primary authority because they are considered advisory only. Courts may, however, find them persuasive if there is no relevant primary

---

18. Cal. Gov't Code §§ 11425.10(a)(7), 11425.60(a) (Deering 2010).

19. Cal. Gov't Code § 11425.60(c) (Deering 2010).

20. Cal. Gov't Code § 11350 authorizes declaratory judgments as to the validity of regulations; Cal. Gov't Code § 11460 authorizes declaratory judgments as to the results of informal agency hearings; Cal. Gov't Code § 11523 authorizes review of the results of formal agency hearings through a writ of mandate.

authority, and in that instance they are "entitled to great weight."[21] An opinion of the attorney general that has stood for a significant period of time may be highly persuasive because courts assume that the legislature was aware of the opinion and could have changed or clarified the law had it disagreed.[22]

Opinions are numbered as they are assigned to be drafted, with a five- or six-digit number that indicates the year and month assigned, and the order in which the opinion was assigned. For example, the opinion responding to the question, "may a city install and utilize an automated photographic traffic enforcement system in order to enforce a right-turn prohibition at an intersection" was assigned the number 11-1104, indicating that it was assigned in 2011 and was the fourth opinion assigned in November.

Attorney general opinions published since 1986 can be located online at oag.ca.gov/opinions. You can perform a search using words, phrases, or the number of a specific opinion. You can also look through the yearly index from 1979 forward, which includes a short summary of each opinion. Finally, there is a Monthly Opinion Report on the site that lists pending assignments and provides links to newly issued opinions.

In print, California attorney general opinions for every year since 1943 have been published in *Opinions of the Attorney General of California*. There is a volume for each year. Each volume contains the text of opinions published in that year, a numerical table of opinions, a table of opinions cited, a table of statutes, and a subject index. Separate indexes were published for the period 1943–1972 and 1973–1982. Since 1983, each volume of *Opinions of the Attorney General of California* includes a cumulative index, with a ten-year cumulative index included at appropriate intervals. For example, the volume for 2012 includes a ten-year cumulative index for 2003–2012.

IV. Federal Administrative Law

The federal government's agencies function much like California's. Agencies such as the Securities and Exchange Commission, the National Labor Relations Board, and the Bureau of Reclamation administer the laws enacted by Congress, promulgate regulations that act like statutes, and adjudicate disputes in quasi-judicial proceedings.

---

21. *Phyle v. Duffy*, 334 U.S. 431, 441 (1948).

22. *Napa Valley Educators' Ass'n v. Napa Valley Unified Sch. Dist.*, 194 Cal. App. 3d 243, 251 (1987).

Figure 8-2. Example of a Federal Regulation

16 C.F.R. § 1507.3 Fuses

TITLE 16 — COMMERCIAL PRACTICES

CHAPTER II — CONSUMER PRODUCT SAFETY COMMISSION

PART 1507 — FIREWORKS DEVICES

Sec. 1507.3 Fuses

(a) Fireworks devices that require a fuse shall:

(1) Utilize only a fuse that has been treated or coated in such manner as to reduce the possibility of side ignition. Devices such as ground spinners that require a restricted orifice for proper thrust and contain less than 6 grams of pyrotechnic composition are exempted from § 1507.3(a)(1).

(2) Utilize only a fuse which will burn at least 3 seconds but not more than 9 seconds before ignition of the device.

(b) The fuse shall be securely attached so that it will support either the weight of the fireworks plus 8 ounces of dead weight or double the weight of the device, whether [sic] is less, without separation from the fireworks device.

Source: *Code of Federal Regulations*, Title 16, Part 1000 to End, pages 539–40 (2008).

The federal APA is codified at 5 U.S.C. § 551 et seq. Its goal is to promote uniformity, public participation, and public confidence in the fairness of the procedures used by agencies of the federal government.

A. *Code of Federal Regulations*

Federal regulations are published in the *Code of Federal Regulations* (C.F.R.), which is published by the Government Publishing Office (GPO). C.F.R. is a codification of regulations issued by all federal agencies. C.F.R. is organized into fifty titles according to agency and subject. Note that the subjects of C.F.R. titles do not all correspond to the subjects of the titles of the United States Code. For example, Title 29 in both U.S.C. and C.F.R. pertains to labor law, but Title 16 of U.S.C. pertains to Conservation, while Title 16 of C.F.R. addresses Commercial Practices. See Figure 8-2 for an example of a federal regulation concerning fireworks.

To research a topic in C.F.R., online or in print, you may use the general index to look up your research terms or the relevant agency's name, and then read the referenced regulations. An easier way to find relevant regulations may be to begin your research in either *United States Code Annotated* (on Westlaw) or *United States Code Service* (on Lexis). Both annotated codes include references to any related regulations for each statutory section. After finding a statute on point, review the annotations following the statutory language for cross-references to regulations. On Lexis or Westlaw, a search in the general query box will retrieve regulations as well as secondary sources, cases, statutes, and other materials.

The annual edition of C.F.R. from 1996 through the present is also available online through the GPO at govinfo.gov/help/cfr. The text there is no more current than the print versions, but the site allows searching by keyword, citation, and title. You can also use the GPO site to access the "Electronic Code of Federal Regulations" (e-CFR). The e-CFR is an unofficial compilation of C.F.R. material and *Federal Register* amendments produced by the National Archives and Records Administration's Office of the Federal Register and the GPO. The e-CFR is updated daily. Finally, the subscription service HeinOnline (heinonline.org) also has a full C.F.R. database in PDF files; if your library subscribes to HeinOnline, you may be able to access C.F.R. through that site.

B. *Federal Register*

New regulations and proposed changes to existing regulations are published first in the *Federal Register*, the federal equivalent of the weekly *California Regulatory Notice Register* (the Z Register). The *Federal Register* publishes all notices of proposed rulemaking, including notices of proposed amendments to existing rules, notices of hearings, responses to public comments on proposed regulations, and helpful tables and indexes. Unlike California's Z Register, the *Federal Register* includes the full text of both proposed and final regulations. The *Federal Register* is the first print source to publish regulations in their final form when they are adopted (i.e., before they are codified in C.F.R.).

The *Federal Register* is published almost every weekday, with continuous pagination throughout the year. Each volume of the *Federal Register* covers a single calendar year, and page numbers reach the tens of thousands in the last few months of the year. The online version of the *Federal Register* covers the years 1936 to the present and is available through govinfo.gov. Lexis and Westlaw also include the *Federal Register* dating back to 1936, as does HeinOnline.

C. Updating Federal Regulations

Lexis and Westlaw provide versions of C.F.R. that are updated to within two weeks of the date on which you look at them. As discussed above, the e-CFR is updated daily. C.F.R. volumes are updated on an annual basis. Updating a federal regulation on the government's website or in print requires the database or booklet called *List of CFR Sections Affected* (LSA); the assistance of a reference librarian is suggested.

D. Decisions of Federal Agencies

Like some California agencies, some federal agencies hold quasi-judicial hearings to decide cases that arise under the agencies' regulations or jurisdiction. Some of these decisions are published in reporters specific to each agency, for example, *Decisions and Orders of the National Labor Relations Board*. A comprehensive list of federal agency reporters is available through the website of Washburn University School of Law at washlaw.edu/doclaw/executive5m.html.

E. Judicial Opinions

The methods of case research explained in Chapter 4 will lead to opinions in which the judiciary reviewed decision of federal agencies. Additionally, C.F.R. can be updated to find relevant cases using Shepard's on Lexis or KeyCite on Westlaw. These citators are addressed in Chapter 9.

Chapter 9

Updating Legal Authority

Ensuring that the authorities found during legal research represent the current law is a critical step in the research process. A few examples demonstrate why: a case decided in 1998 may have subsequently been overruled, a case decided last year may have been reversed on appeal, and a recently enacted statute may have just been declared unconstitutional. These three authorities would still appear in online and print sources, but they should not be relied on in legal analysis. Determining whether an authority is current and respected is called *updating*.[1]

Updating an authority requires determining how each legal source that has subsequently cited that authority treated it on a particular issue. A *citator* provides a list of citations to those sources that cite your authority.

Citators are also valuable tools for expanding research. By reading cases that have cited a relevant authority, you can quickly find other authorities on the same topic. Citators also list secondary sources, which can provide insight into the authority you are updating. Thus, citators are valuable both for updating and as research tools.

I. Citator Fundamentals

The leading online providers of legal material both have extensive citator services. *Shepard's* is the online citator available on Lexis; Westlaw's citator is called *KeyCite*.[2] Their coverage of California material is not identical, though

---

1. This step is sometimes referred to as "Shepardizing" because the first major updating tool was a print series called *Shepard's Citations*. Many law libraries no longer maintain the print series.

2. Other online legal research providers also have citators: "BCite" on Bloomberg Law, "V.Cite" on VersusLaw, "How cited" on Google Scholar, "CASEcheck" on Casemaker, and "Authority Check" on Fastcase. None rivals KeyCite or Shepard's, though some offer less expensive alternatives.

Table 9-1. Updating Outline

---

1. Access the list of citing sources (typically by clicking on a link or symbol, or by entering the citation of the cited source in a search box).

2. Select the type of citation list needed:
    - a short list for validating the cited source (to examine any negative treatment by later cases),
    - an extensive list of all citing sources for expanding your research,
    - a list of sources referred to in the cited source (called a Table of Authorities).

3. Evaluate the analytical symbols provided by the citator.

4. Limit the citator results by jurisdiction, headnote, date, or other function.

5. Prioritize and read the citing sources.
    - Analyze the impact, if any, that primary authorities have on the validity of the cited source.
    - Consider whether citing cases are helpful to your research and whether citing secondary sources add to your understanding of the cited source.

---

both cover cases, statutes, constitutional provisions, regulations, and some secondary sources.[3]

A. Updating Process

The process of updating online is summarized in Table 9-1. In that table, the *cited source* is the document you are updating. In much of this chapter, the cited source will be a case. The *citing sources* (or *citing references*) are documents in the lists you generate through updating. This chapter explains how to locate lists of citing sources and how to use them efficiently to validate and expand your research.

B. Reading Lists of Citing Sources

The principal work of a citator is to provide lists of sources referring to the document, like a case, that you are updating. You determine which of these

---

3. The "Scope" link provides updated information about KeyCite coverage. The "Scope" link is located toward the bottom of the main KeyCite webpage. Shepard's provides a "Product Guide" that is available from the Shepard's tab by clicking the "Help" link.

sources warrant reading and decide for yourself whether your case is still "good law." The citator uses symbols to show you how a source treats your case (e.g., follows, distinguishes, overrules) that can alert you to possible problems. Skim these symbols to determine which sources to read and to decide the impact of a source on the case you want to use in your analysis. Do not rely thoughtlessly on the symbols. A cautionary yellow symbol might mean only that your case has been criticized by courts in another jurisdiction. Even a red symbol does not necessarily indicate that the case should not be cited; it might have been overruled on a point of law unrelated to your research.

To review a source that might affect the validity of your case, simply click on the source to go to the point in the source that cites your case. Quickly skim that portion of the source. If it is relevant to your research, read the citing source carefully and analyze its impact on your case: Does the source reverse your case, perhaps meaning that the rule of law has changed or that a certain set of facts did not satisfy the law? Does the source follow your case, simply applying the law to a new fact pattern? If the source distinguishes or criticizes your case, ask why and how. Sometimes a citing source does not address the legal question at issue in your research project; in that instance, disregard that source.

Reading and analyzing the citing sources provides research benefits beyond determining whether the cited case is still "good law." A citing source may have facts more similar to your client's situation. A court may make a point in a particularly helpful way. Or a citing source may raise a related claim that you had not previously considered.

C. Prioritizing and Narrowing Results

Unless the list of citing sources is very short, reading every source included on the list would rarely be an effective exercise. Instead, prioritize the citing sources you will read according to the following criteria:

- *Negative treatment.* Look for any case that reverses, overrules, criticizes, or distinguishes your case.
- *Jurisdiction.* Prioritize cases from your jurisdiction.
- *Hierarchy.* Read cases from the highest appellate court, then the intermediate appellate courts, and finally the trial courts (if trial court cases are published) in your jurisdiction.
- *Date.* Start with more recent cases.
- *Headnotes.* Prioritize citing sources that refer to the headnotes from the cited case that are on point for your research.

Use filters, often provided in the left margin of a screen, to narrow the citing sources to those most important to your project. Common filters include date, jurisdiction, judge, and whether the citing sources treat your cited source positively or negatively.

D. Setting Alerts

KeyCite and Shepard's allow you to set "Alert" functions to notify you of action on an authority that you have updated. A bell icon is often used for this function. You can customize the information you want to receive (e.g., negative action on a particular headnote) and determine how often you want to receive notice (e.g., daily, weekly), during what period (e.g., the next month), and through what method (e.g., email).

II. Updating Cases

The next few pages explain how to update cases using KeyCite and Shepard's. Regardless of the service you use, the updating process involves the five steps introduced in Table 9-1. After these five steps, you should have a focused list of results to study and read, as explained above.

A. KeyCite on Westlaw

1. Access the Citator

Westlaw automatically generates KeyCite information for each case that you open. The top of the Westlaw screen displaying a case has links for the different citing lists: Negative Treatment, History, Citing References, and Table of Authorities. An alternative for accessing KeyCite is to type "KC" followed by the case citation in the main search box on Westlaw's home page.

2. Select the Type of Citing List

Negative Treatment shows any negative impact from cases in the same litigation or any negative references from other cases (i.e., in different litigation). History includes all cases in the same litigation, whether they had a positive or negative impact on the case you are updating. The History cases are available in both list and graphical format. The Citing References list shows all cases not in the same litigation that have cited the case you are updating; thus, there is overlap with the cases in Negative Treatment. Finally, the Table of Authorities

Table 9-2. Symbols for Updating Cases with KeyCite

KeyCite Symbol	Meaning
Red flag	Case has negative treatment; the case is no longer good law for at least one point, e.g., at least a portion of the case has been reversed or overruled
Yellow flag	Case has some negative treatment, but has not been reversed or overruled
Orange !	Case is at risk of being overruled because it relies on authority that is invalid or has itself been overruled
Blue/white flag	A federal case has an appeal pending
Green bars	Depth of treatment (how much space the citing reference devotes to your case)
Green quotation marks	The citing reference quotes your case

lists the cases cited by your case; it is a retrospective look at those cases your case relied on.

3. Analyze the Citator Symbols

The citator symbols used for Westlaw are summarized in Table 9-2. A pop-up box explaining the symbols appears when you click on "Powered by KeyCite."

4. Limit the Search Results

Westlaw provides many options for how to view and narrow the Citing References. See Figure 9-1. From a drop-down menu, you can choose to view results organized by date (most recent or oldest first) or by depth of treatment. In the left margin, you can view the results by document type by clicking on cases, secondary sources, appellate court documents, etc. Moreover, you can filter the results by search term, jurisdiction, date, depth of treatment, headnote, treatment status, and whether the citing reference is a reported or an unreported case. A "+" symbol next to a filtering option opens more possibilities, for example listing all of the federal or state jurisdictions in which courts have cited your case. Regardless of which filters you apply, be sure to read the citing references that seem most applicable to your project. Evaluate their impact on your case (to determine if your case is still good law), and consider whether they add to your analysis (perhaps by explaining a point particularly well).

Figure 9-1. KeyCite on Westlaw Edge: Narrowing Citing References

Source: Westlaw. Used with permission of Thomson Reuters..

B. Shepard's on Lexis

1. Access the Citator

You can access Shepard's on Lexis in two ways:

- by typing "shep:" and a citation into the main search box, and
- from any document with a Shepard's symbol or a "Shepardize" link, by clicking on that symbol or link.

2. Select the Type of Citing List

Shepard's typically provides four lists of citing references for a judicial opinion, each with its own link: Appellate History; Citing Decisions; Other

Figure 9-2. *Shepard's*® on Lexis Advance®

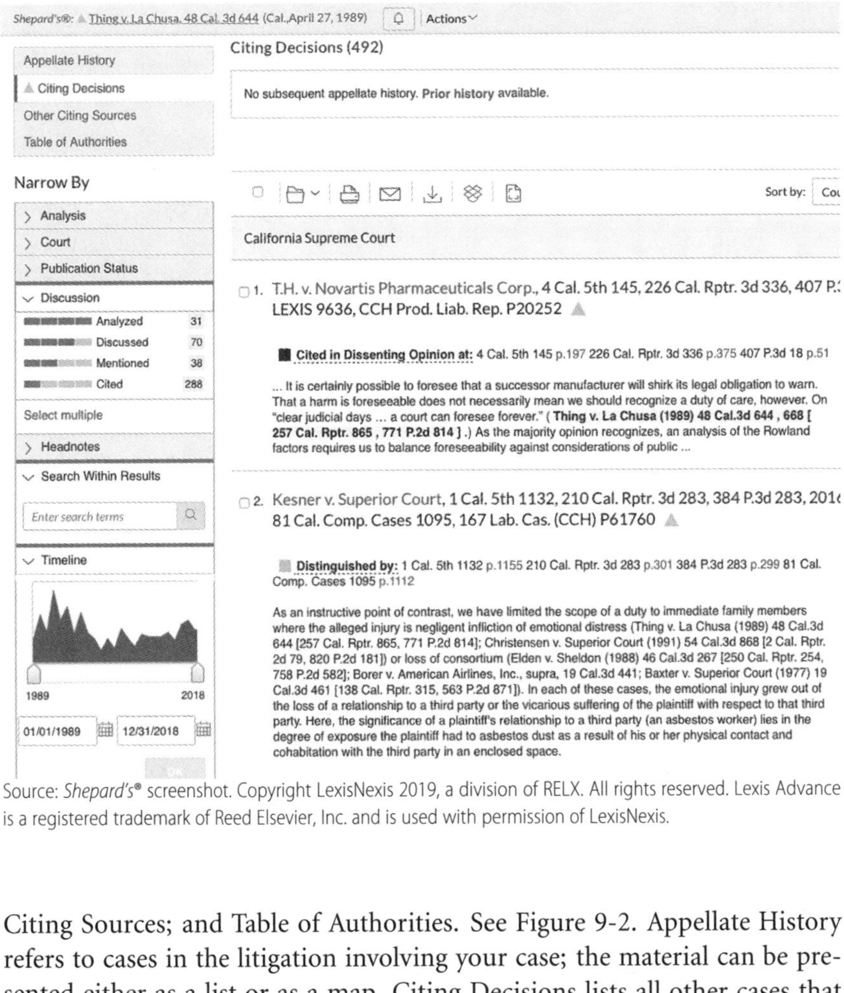

Source: *Shepard's*® screenshot. Copyright LexisNexis 2019, a division of RELX. All rights reserved. Lexis Advance® is a registered trademark of Reed Elsevier, Inc. and is used with permission of LexisNexis.

Citing Sources; and Table of Authorities. See Figure 9-2. Appellate History refers to cases in the litigation involving your case; the material can be presented either as a list or as a map. Citing Decisions lists all other cases that have cited your case, while secondary sources and court briefs are listed under Other Citing Sources. The final link, Table of Authorities, lists all of the cases cited by your case. The Table of Authorities looks back to list the cases your case relied on; in contrast, the other lists look forward from your case to future cases that cite it.

3. Analyze the Citator Symbols

A "Legend" link at the bottom right of each list explains the colored analytical symbols used by Shepard's. In the Shepard's list, each symbol is accompanied by a word or phrase explaining its significance; the colors simply provide a quick visual overview.

- Red warns of negative treatment (e.g., your case has been reversed or overruled).
- Orange questions the continuing validity of the case, while yellow indicates some serious negative impact (e.g., your case has been criticized).
- Green shows positive treatment (e.g., the later case affirmed or followed your case).
- Blue suggests neutral treatment, which could mean your case was explained or that it was discussed in a concurring or dissenting opinion.

In addition to the symbols showing the type of analysis provided by the Citing Decisions, a set of bars show the "Depth of Discussion" of your case. Four bars means that your case was analyzed, three bars means it was discussed, two bars means it was mentioned, and one bar means that it was merely cited. In most instances, you can prioritize cases that have analyzed or discussed your case.

To the right of the name of each citing decision in the list, another colored symbol shows the subsequent treatment of that citing decision. See Figure 9-2. If a citing decision has itself been reversed, then it might not be as significant for your research. Lexis does not include in its list of citing decisions court of appeal cases that were never published. If the supreme court granted or denied review and then ordered a case to be not published or depublished, however, that case may appear in the list of citing sources.

4. Limit the Search Results

You can manipulate the data in the list to concentrate on the citing references that are most useful for your project. For example, using a drop-down menu at the far right of the list of Citing Decisions, you can organize the list by court, date, type of analysis (red to blue), and depth of discussion (analyzed to cited). As another example, you can use the "Grid" link at the top right of the Citing Decisions page to view the cases on colored grids. One grid arranges the cases by type of analysis and court, while another grid arranges them by analysis and date.

In the left margin, you can narrow the search results using a number of filters: analysis, court, depth of discussion, headnotes, search terms, and date (using the timeline filter).

Figure 9-3. Statute Updating on KeyCite with Westlaw Edge

🏴 § 340.5. Action against health care provider; three years from injury or
CA CIV PRO § 340.5 · West's Annotated California Codes · Code of Civil Procedure (Approx. 2 pages)

Document   Notes of Decisions (304)   **History (12) ▾**   Citing References (10,037) ▾   Context & Analysis

KeyCite. Validity (4)

☐ Select all items · No items selected

Case Treatment (4)
Limited on Constitutional Grounds by

☐ 🏴 Photias v. Doerfler
   53 Cal.Rptr.2d 202, 202+, (Cal.App. 2 Dist. May 22, 1996), (NO. B091837)

☐ 🏴 Torres v. County of Los Angeles
   257 Cal.Rptr. 211, 211+, (Cal.App. 2 Dist. Apr. 03, 1989), (NO. B027019)

☐ 🏴 Young v. Haines
   226 Cal.Rptr. 547, 547+, (Cal. June 05, 1986), (NO. S.F. 24775)

Limitation Recognized by

☐ Arredondo v. Regents of University of California
   31 Cal.Rptr.3d 800, 800+, (Cal.App. 2 Dist. July 27, 2005), (NO. B176881)

Source: Westlaw. Used with permission of Thomson Reuters.

III. Updating Statutes

The basic process of updating statutes with KeyCite and Shepard's is the same as the process of updating cases: enter a citation on the appropriate screen (or click on the appropriate symbol while viewing the statute), review the sources listed, examine the analytical symbols (if any), restrict the search, and read the citing sources.

As with cases, both services provide more than one list for updating statutes. KeyCite in Westlaw provides History, Citing References, and Context & Analysis. See Figure 9-3. On Lexis, the three lists available for statutes are History, Citing Decisions, and Other Citing Sources.

Both KeyCite and Shepard's provide colored symbols that suggest the validity of the statute; the precise meaning of each symbol is different from when the symbol refers to cases. For example, on KeyCite a red flag for a statute may mean that the statute has been amended, repealed, superseded, held unconstitutional, or preempted. Shepard's includes a unique symbol for statutes, an exclamation point noting negative case treatment.

IV. Updating Other Authorities

Many authorities from other federal and state jurisdictions can be updated online, including regulations and secondary sources. KeyCite and Shepard's are expanding their coverage, so check frequently for current information.

Chapter 10

Secondary Sources

I. Introduction

As noted in Chapter 1, primary sources of law like statutes, cases, and regulations are produced by legislatures, courts, and administrative agencies; secondary sources are written by law professors, practicing attorneys, legal editors, and law students. Only primary sources may be binding, but secondary sources are invaluable in legal research, especially when researching an unfamiliar area of law. Although this book covers secondary sources after primary sources, the research process outlined in Chapter 1 includes research in secondary sources as the second step.

Lawyers use secondary sources for two reasons: to learn about the law and to find references to relevant primary authority. Beginning a new research project — even on a familiar topic — with a secondary source may be the most effective approach. A secondary source may provide an overview of the pertinent issues or a deep analysis of the relevant question. A secondary source may also explain terminology and concepts, making it possible to develop a more effective list of research terms. Finally, secondary sources often aid in locating relevant primary authority by citing cases, statutes, and regulations.

Not all secondary sources are equally authoritative. Some are so well respected that courts cite them, even though they are not authoritative in the way that a statute or other primary authority is. Other secondary sources are highly regarded for their ability to aid in research and understanding legal issues, but would rarely if ever be cited. Lawyers also distinguish between those secondary sources that are more theoretical, such as law review articles, and those that are more practice-oriented, which are sometimes referred to as "practice guides."

This chapter includes the most widely used and most fundamental secondary sources:

- the Witkin series, a source unique to California legal research;
- legal encyclopedias;
- practice guides, treatises, and other books;
- legal periodicals, including law reviews and bar journals;
- *American Law Reports*;
- continuing legal education (CLE) publications;
- legal forms;
- restatements and principles, published by the American Law Institute;
- uniform laws and model codes;
- jury instructions; and
- library guides.

The chapter concludes with a discussion of when and how to use secondary sources in legal research.

As an initial matter, some researchers prefer secondary sources in print, rather than the online version. This preference especially holds true when researching a complicated issue in an unfamiliar area of law. However, many of the secondary sources discussed in this chapter can be found on Lexis, Westlaw, and other online services. Some secondary sources are available for free on state websites. A list of helpful websites for California research is provided in Table 10-1. In addition, a quick search on Google or other search engines may produce valuable leads. A law firm's website may provide helpful summaries of the law or a useful collection of statutory references. However, before relying on these sources, consider the questions raised at the end of this chapter. A law librarian is often the best resource for learning of relevant secondary sources and how to use them.

Table 10-1. Selected Websites for Research in California Secondary Sources

Website	Address	Secondary Sources
California State Bar	calbar.ca.gov	*California Bar Journal* and CLE materials
California Judicial Branch	courts.ca.gov/forms.htm	Forms
California Jury Instructions	courts.ca.gov/partners/ juryinstructions.htm	Jury instructions
The Recorder	therecorder.com	Legal news
Law360	law360.com	Legal news

Figure 10-1. Excerpt from Witkin on "Contracts"

[§ 179] Binding Purchase Agreement.

Whether an instrument creates an option or a contract of sale is determined not by its title or form, but by an analysis of the obligations imposed. (*Scarbery v. Bill Patch Land & Water Co.* (1960) 184 C.A.2d 87, 100, 7 C.R. 408; *Welk v. Fainbarg* (1967) 255 C.A.2d 269, 276, 63 C.R. 127 [held only an option].)

In *People v. Ocean Shore R. Co.* (1949) 90 C.A.2d 464, 203 P.2d 579, K made an agreement with M, entitled "option," under which M was given "the exclusive right and option to purchase" certain property on stated installments, with the proviso that on default in an installment K could cancel and retain prior payments, but that K otherwise "shall have no right or claim against" M. *Held*, the agreement was merely an option and not a contract of sale. Despite the fact that M took possession and made regular payments, the language of the instrument showed a studious avoidance of any commitment by M to pay the purchase price, and he could not have been compelled to perform. (90 C.A.2d 469.) (For disapproval of *Ocean Shore* on the issue of whether an option is a compensable interest in condemnation, see 8 *Summary* (11th), *Constitutional Law*, § 1267.)

Source: 1 B.E. Witkin, *Summary of California Law* Contracts § 179 (11th ed. 2018). Reprinted with permission of the B.E. Witkin Article Sixth Testamentary Trust.

II. Witkin's *Summary of California Law*

One of the most widely used and highly regarded secondary sources in California is B.E. Witkin's *Summary of California Law*, which is usually referred to simply as "Witkin."[1] While some researchers refer to it as a "treatise" and others think of it as an "encyclopedia," it is a unique resource that California lawyers frequently consult. Witkin concisely summarizes and examines California statutes and case law. Figure 10-1 contains an excerpt from Witkin.

Witkin is available on Westlaw and Lexis. In print, Witkin is divided into sixteen volumes. Some of them contain only one subject, while others contain a number of subjects. The subjects appear in numbered volumes in the following order:

1. Contracts
2. Insurance; Workers' Compensation
3. Agency and Employment

---

1. The Witkin Legal Institute also publishes other, more specialized surveys such as *California Criminal Law*, *California Evidence*, and *California Procedure*.

4. Sales; Negotiable Instruments; Secured Transactions in Personal Property; Security Transactions in Real Property
5. Torts
6. Torts
7. Constitutional Law
8. Constitutional Law
9. Taxation; Partnerships; Corporations
10. Parent and Child
11. Husband and Wife; Community Property
12. Real Property
13. Personal Property; Equity; Trusts
14. Wills and Probate

Volume 15 contains tables, and volume 16 is the index for all the volumes. To find an entry, review the softbound index volume using your research terms.

III. Legal Encyclopedias

Legal encyclopedias provide general information on a wide variety of legal subjects. They are organized by subject matter under *topics*, broad subject matter areas like Employer and Employee, Family Law, and Landlord and Tenant. Topics are presented alphabetically in bound volumes and online. California's encyclopedia is *California Jurisprudence, Third Edition* (Cal. Jur. 3d),[2] though some also consider Witkin an encyclopedia. Only larger states, like California, have an encyclopedia dedicated to that state's law.

Cal. Jur. 3d is available online on both Westlaw and Lexis. To use Cal. Jur. 3d in print, review the softbound index volumes for your research terms. The references will include both an abbreviated word or phrase — the topic — and a section number.[3] The encyclopedia's topic abbreviations are explained in tables in the front of the index volumes. Select the bound volume containing a relevant topic and skim the material at the beginning of that topic for an overview. Then, turn to the particular section number given in the index and read the text there. Pocket parts — pages inserted in the back cover of a book — sometimes provide updated commentary.

---

2. The two national legal encyclopedias are *Corpus Juris Secundum* (C.J.S.) and *American Jurisprudence, Second Edition* (Am. Jur. 2d).

3. These topics and section numbers are distinct from the West digest system of topics and key numbers, which were discussed in Chapter 4.

The text of most encyclopedia entries is cursory because the writer's goal is to summarize the law. In addition to describing the law, legal encyclopedias also provide citations to primary authority. California encyclopedias cite California primary authority. In Cal. Jur. 3d, cases and statutes appear in footnotes accompanying the text. Be sure to check the footnotes for recent, primary authority.[4]

An encyclopedia may also contain cross-references to other sources, especially those produced by the same publisher. For example, Cal. Jur. 3d includes cross-references to relevant topics and key numbers in West's digests.

IV. Practice Guides, Treatises, and Other Books

A book on a legal topic can provide an in-depth discussion of the topic and relevant references to primary authority. Legal texts include practice guides, treatises, hornbooks, *Nutshells*, and monographs. Each type of book covers a particular legal subject, such as contracts or civil procedure or business law, but they are written for different audiences and serve different purposes.

Practice guides typically cover an area of law thoroughly, focusing on the nuts and bolts of practice. They are particularly helpful to attorneys learning about unfamiliar areas of law. Both treatises and hornbooks present a more theoretical approach than do practice guides, but treatises are generally more comprehensive. Thus, a treatise might be useful to an attorney with a particularly challenging question, while hornbooks are more often used by law students. *Nutshells* are also more commonly used by students because they offer a condensed explanation of the law. In just a few hundred pages, a *Nutshell* might give an overview of tort law, insurance law, or real property law. Monographs are single volumes that provide in-depth and original analysis of focused topics. Of all legal books, monographs are least likely to be available online. This chapter focuses on practice guides and treatises because they are more commonly used in practice than hornbooks and *Nutshells* and because they have characteristics unique from monographs and other books.

---

4. Because the footnotes in the national encyclopedias, C.J.S. and Am. Jur. 2d, cite to authorities from all American jurisdictions and tend to be dated, the chance of finding a reference to a recent, relevant case from your jurisdiction in either of them is limited.

Table 10-2. Selected Practice Guide Topics

Selected CEB Practice Guides	Selected Rutter Group Practice Guides
California Estate Planning	Alternative Dispute Resolution
California Juvenile Dependency Practice	Bankruptcy
	Civil Procedure Before Trial
California Land Use Practice	Corporations
California Tort Damages	Federal Civil Procedure Before Trial
Internet Law and Practice in California	Landlord-Tenant
	Sentencing California Crimes
Organizing Corporations in California	
Wrongful Employment Termination Practice: Discrimination, Harassment & Retaliation	

A. California Practice Guides

California lawyers rely heavily on practice guides. Each one covers one area of law in depth. The authors are typically judges or practitioners with extensive experience in the legal area they are writing about, and the text is practice-oriented. Table 10-2 provides a selected list of practice guide topics.

Of the four major providers of practice guides in California,[5] The Rutter Group is the most highly regarded in many areas of law. Its guides—often called "Rutter Guides"—are written by judges, justices, and lawyers.[6] If there is a Rutter Guide on your issue, it is almost always guaranteed to provide excellent guidance. Figure 10-2 shows an excerpt from a Rutter Guide.

The other three providers of practice guides are Continuing Education of the Bar (CEB), a joint enterprise of the State Bar of California and the University of California, which is the largest publisher of practice guides in California; Bancroft-Whitney; and Matthew Bender. In addition to traditional practice guides, CEB publishes *Action Guides*, which provide lists of procedures for attorneys to follow in very specific situations, such as "Handling Motions to Compel" or "Obtaining a Writ of Attachment." In addition to these providers,

---

5. National scope practice guides are published by the Practising Law Institute (PLI), the American Law Institute (ALI), and the American Bar Association (ABA).

6. The Rutter Group also produces practice guides for areas of federal law.

Figure 10-2. Excerpt from Rutter Group Practice Guide: Civil Trials and Evidence*

---

c.   [8:460] Effect of alteration of object: Admissibility may be affected where the object has been altered in some way between the time of the incident in question and trial. In each case, the court must determine whether such alterations affect the object's authenticity. The court may decide that the probative value of the object is outweighed by risks of confusing or misleading the jury. [Ev.C. § 352, *see detailed discussion in Ch. 8F*]

(1)   [8:461] **Adverse inference from destruction or concealment**: The reasons for the alteration are significant. Deliberate attempts to conceal or destroy evidence may result in adverse inferences against the responsible party: "[A] party's … suppression of evidence by … spoliation…, is receivable against him as an indication of his consciousness *that his case is a weak or unfounded one*." [*Thor v. Boska* (1974) 38 CA3d 558, 567, 113 CR 296, 302 (emphasis added; internal quotes omitted); see *Cedars-Sinai Med. Ctr. v. Sup.Ct. (Bowyer)* (1998) 18 C4th 1, 12, 74 CR2d 248, 254; see also CACI 204 (willful suppression of evidence instruction)]

[8:461.1] ***PRACTICE POINTERS***: Instruct clients *firmly and clearly in writing* against destruction of any potential evidence relevant to ongoing or anticipated litigation.

Exercise caution when advising clients about removal of information from social media web pages. Emphasize to the clients that they should print and save a screen shot of any relevant information and also copy the electronic version of the information to another server for preservation before deleting it.

(2)   [8:462] **Compare — innocent alterations**: Often, however, there are reasonable explanations for the alterations: For example, the object may have been damaged in the accident or altered in the course of testing by experts.

Source: Reprinted with permission of The Rutter Group, a Thomson Reuters business from Wegner, Fairbank, Epstein & Chernow, CAL. PRAC. GUIDE: CIVIL TRIALS & EVIDENCE (The Rutter Group 2018). All rights reserved.

* The authors of this Rutter Group Practice Guide are William E. Wegner, Gibson, Dunn & Crutcher LLP, Los Angeles; Robert H. Fairbank, Fairbank & Vincent, Los Angeles; Justice Norman L. Epstein, California Court of Appeal, 2d Dist.; and Judge Eli Chernow (Ret.), Los Angeles Superior Court.

the California State Bar publishes some practice guides. For a list of the Bar's publications, visit the Bar's website at calbar.ca.gov.

Almost all practice guides available in print are also available online through either Westlaw or Lexis. Rutter Group and Bancroft-Whitney guides are available only on Westlaw, while Matthew Bender guides are available only on Lexis.[7] In print, many practice guides, including the Rutter Guides, are published in looseleaf binders to allow for easy updating by replacing outdated pages. Some guides are published in hardbound volumes and updated with pocket parts. Still others are republished in full when they need to be updated. Always be sure that you are using the most current material available by checking the library catalog and browsing the shelves nearby.

B. Treatises

Treatises can be excellent starting points for research. An example of a highly regarded treatise with a California focus is Miller & Starr's *California Real Estate*. Consider asking a law librarian or a colleague if there is a well-known treatise for the topic you are researching.

Treatises are typically available online and in print. Online, the Lexis sources under "Treatises" often offer broad overviews, analysis of specific issues, and footnotes with cites to related primary authority. To find treatises on Westlaw, click on "Secondary Sources" and then on "Texts & Treatises."

C. Finding and Using Legal Books

Practice guides, treatises, hornbooks, and *Nutshells* can be located by searching the library catalog for the general subject matter of a research project. For a well-known treatise, include the author's name as one of the search terms. When searching for practice-oriented material, use the name of the publisher (e.g., Continuing Education of the Bar or American Law Institute). Recognize that a number of legal books are available only in print format. After finding one book on point in the library, scan the other titles shelved around it for additional resources.

To use legal books for research, begin with either the table of contents or the index. In multi-volume treatises, the index is often in the last volume of the series. Locate your research terms and record the references given. A reference may be to a page number, section number, or paragraph number, depending on the publisher. Once you locate and read the relevant text, note any pertinent primary authority cited in the footnotes.

---

7. Although Bloomberg Law does not have many of the general practice guides commonly used by California attorneys, it has a number of subject-specific practice guides and other resources commonly used in areas such as tax, transactional, corporate, securities, environmental, and health law.

The authoritative value of a book depends on the intended audience, the depth of analysis, and the reputation of the author. For example, the well-regarded treatise *Marsh's California Corporation Law* comprises four volumes with chapters devoted to issues ranging from corporate formation to shareholders' right. One of the authors is a partner in the high-profile California-based law firm of Allen Matkins. In contrast, a *Nutshell* on corporations is designed as a study guide for students or a quick overview for practitioners; it is not considered authoritative.

V. Legal Periodicals

A. Law Reviews and Law Journals

Law reviews and law journals contain articles that address specific legal issues in detail. An article may be authored by a law professor, judge, practitioner, or student. Because the author is not constrained by representing a client's interests or deciding a particular case, an article can explore the law critically and propose changes.

Reading articles published in law reviews and journals can provide a thorough understanding of current law because authors often explain existing law before making their recommendations. Articles may also identify weaknesses or new trends in the law that might address your client's situation. And the many footnotes in law review and law journal articles can provide excellent summaries of relevant research.

Although not as authoritative as articles written by recognized experts, student articles can provide clear and careful analysis, and their footnotes are valuable research tools. Articles written by students are called "Notes" or "Comments." Students also author shorter law review pieces called "Case Notes" or "Recent Developments," which summarize a recent case that the publication's editors consider important.

There are generally two kinds of law reviews or law journals — those that are published by law students and those that are "peer-edited," meaning that law professors select and edit the articles. Most law reviews and law journals are published by law students who were selected to run the journal based on their grades or through a writing competition. Many of these student law reviews have general audiences and cover a broad range of topics; an example is the *McGeorge Law Review*. Other student-run law journals focus on a specific area of law; examples include the *Hastings Race and Poverty Law Journal*, the *Loyola of Los Angeles Entertainment Law Review*, and the *Berkeley Journal of*

International Law. Peer-edited law journals tend to focus on a specific area of the law. Examples of this type of law journal include the *Journal of Legal Education* and *Legal Communication & Rhetoric: JALWD.*

Law reviews and law journals are located by volume number, the name of the journal, and the first page of the article. While some law reviews and law journals are available both online and in print, many have moved to online publication only. Articles may be located on the law journals' websites as well as on Lexis, Westlaw, Bloomberg Law, HeinOnline, Google Scholar, and other online services.

Unlike other secondary sources, law review and law journal articles do not need to be "updated." Once an article is published, neither the author nor the publisher changes or adds to the text to keep it current. You can, however, find out whether an article has been cited favorably or unfavorably by using a citator, as explained in Chapter 9.

B. Bar Journals

Like other state bars, the California State Bar publishes a monthly journal, the *California Bar Journal*, with articles aimed at attorneys practicing in the state.[8] Many of the larger county bar associations also have monthly publications with similar articles. Examples include the Los Angeles County Bar Association and the San Francisco County Bar Association. Articles in state and county bar journals are often shorter than articles published in law reviews and do not have the extensive footnotes found in law review articles.

C. Locating Articles

Full-text searching for law reviews and law journals is available on Westlaw, Lexis, and other services, and more sophisticated search engines can return accurate results. Techniques discussed in Chapter 2 of this text are effective for searching for articles and filtering results.

HeinOnline offers full-text searching of a large number of journal articles, although it does not generally contain articles published within the preceding two years. The search engine is not as sophisticated as Lexis or Westlaw, but it can be effective. One advantage to retrieving articles from HeinOnline is

---

8. The American Bar Association publishes the *ABA Journal*, which has articles of general interest to attorneys across the nation.

that the text is provided in PDF format, meaning that pagination looks exactly like the print copy (which makes citation of pinpoint pages easier) and footnotes accompany the relevant text (rather than being placed at the end of the article). Many law school libraries subscribe to HeinOnline, making it free to students and patrons. The website is heinonline.org.

Another free site is Google Scholar. It indexes a vast number of articles on a broad array of scholarly topics. To open an article, the researcher is usually linked to a site like HeinOnline. Other linked sites include ERIC (the Education Resources Information Center) and SSRN (formerly called the Social Science Research Network). SSRN includes articles that have not yet been published, making it a good source for information on cutting edge issues.[9]

VI. *American Law Reports*

American Law Reports (A.L.R.) contains lengthy articles (until recently called "annotations") and extensive research aids.[10] Articles address discrete topics and, unlike law review articles, they are practice-oriented. The content of the articles is highly regarded for research, but the authors are not recognized experts. Rarely would you cite an A.L.R. article. The research aids that accompany each article include tables and graphs with exhaustive information on the law of various jurisdictions.

Figure 10-3 shows an excerpt from an A.L.R. article that explores one requirement for recovery under the tort "negligent infliction of emotional distress" — the immediacy of the bystander's perception of the accident. This is the cause of action for the client issue discussed in Chapter 1. The article begins with an outline, research references, an index of topics covered, and a table of relevant cases from various jurisdictions, including a lengthy list of California cases.

A.L.R. has been published in multiple series. Currently, *A.L.R.3d* through *A.L.R.7th* address state law issues, *A.L.R. Federal* covers federal law issues, and *A.L.R. International* is devoted to global issues. The first two numbered series

---

9. Periodical indexes have traditionally offered the most accurate way of locating relevant articles in print. These indexes use specific subject headings under which various articles are classified. Two of the more popular indexes of legal periodicals are the *Current Law Index* (CLI) and the *Index to Legal Periodicals and Books* (ILPB).

10. Until recently, A.L.R. was a hybrid resource, in that it provided not only articles but also full-length cases that were relevant to those articles.

Figure 10-3. A.L.R. Annotation

Immediacy of Observation of Injury as Affecting Right to Recover Damages for Shock or Mental Anguish from Wi...
American Law Reports ALR5th   Originally published in 2002   (Approx. 91 pages)

| Document | History (2) | Citing References (79) | ▾ | Table of Authorities | Powered by KeyCite |

99 A.L.R.5th 301 (Originally published in 2002)

American Law Reports
ALR5th

The ALR databases are made current by the weekly addition of relevant new cases.

Immediacy of Observation of Injury as Affecting Right to Recover Damages for Shock or Mental Anguish from
Witnessing Injury to Another

Dale Joseph Gilsinger, J.D.

One criterion used to determine whether a bystander can recover for emotional distress upon witnessing injury to another is the immediacy of the bystander's sensory observation of the injury, that is, the temporal and spatial proximity between the injury–producing event and the bystander's sensory observation of the victim's injured state. In stating the test for bystander recovery, many courts have attempted to formulate the requisite degree of immediacy by requiring that the bystander contemporaneously observe the injury–causing event or its immediate aftermath. The application of this requirement has frequently necessitated the analysis of particular circumstances to determine whether the bystander's observation of injury was sufficiently proximate to the injury–causing event. For example, in Groves v. Taylor, 729 N.E.2d 569, 99 A.L.R.5th 693 (Ind. 2000), the court determined that the jurisdiction's criteria for bystander recovery, including the requirement that the plaintiff actually witness or arrive on the scene soon after the death or severe injury of a loved one, were satisfied where an eight–year–old girl heard the sound of a car colliding with the body of her six–year–old brother and turned to witness his body as it rolled away from the point of impact. This annotation collects and analyzes cases applying the immediacy of observation of injury requirement to determine recovery for emotional distress due to witnessing injury to another.

TABLE OF CONTENTS
Article Outline
Index
Table of Cases, Laws, and Rules
Research References

contained both state and federal subjects. Note that earlier series still contain helpful information and updates are added regularly.

The complete A.L.R. set is available on Westlaw. Lexis does not provide *A.L.R.1st* and as of this writing includes only through *A.L.R.6th* in the state series and *A.L.R. Fed 2d* in the federal series. Articles and research aids are updated regularly on both Westlaw and Lexis. To locate an A.L.R. series in your library, search the library catalog for *American Law Reports*. Often, the most effective tool for locating annotations using A.L.R. in print is a single-volume Quick Index for the series you wish to search. Alternatively, search the A.L.R Index, a multi-volume reference that covers the more recent numbered series and the federal series together. Another search tool is West's A.L.R. Digest, which includes references to annotations, practice aids, and A.L.R. cases. A.L.R. annotations are updated with pocket parts. Also check the Annotation History Table in the A.L.R. Index volumes to see whether an annotation has been supplemented or superseded by another annotation, rather than just updated in pocket parts.

VII. Continuing Legal Education Publications

Attorneys in California are required to complete twenty-five hours of minimum continuing legal education (MCLE) courses every three years to maintain their membership in the State Bar. MCLE courses are led by presenters with significant practice or academic experience, and any course longer than one hour must include written materials. These materials could include sample forms, sample documents, and explanations of the law. While these materials may have very useful information, they may not be readily available to those who did not take the course. Some of the common California-based providers of continuing legal education (CLE) materials are the state and local bar associations.[11] Locate CLE material by searching for the provider online. Or, to find CLE material in print, search in the library catalog by topic or by author, using the names of the more common CLE publishers as search terms.

---

11. Some of the largest national publishers of similar CLE materials are the Practising Law Institute (PLI), the American Law Institute (ALI), and the American Bar Association (ABA).

VIII. Forms

Forms provide shortcuts in legal drafting. When you are drafting a document for the first time in an unfamiliar area of law, a form provides an excellent starting point by suggesting language that might be appropriate or by showing requirements of a court or statute. Forms are available from a diverse range of sources. The best form is often a document drafted by someone else in your law office on a similar topic.[12] Both Lexis and Westlaw provide access to forms on many topics.

The website of the California judiciary contains links to forms created and approved by the California Judicial Council. The forms cover matters ranging from domestic violence to probate. They are downloadable from the California courts' website at courts.ca.gov/forms. Forms are also available on some superior court websites. For example, the Los Angeles Superior Court's website, lacourt.org, has several links to forms.

California statutes provide forms for some situations. To find statutory forms, search the code index both for the substantive content of the form and under the term "forms." Legal forms may also be found in court rules (introduced in Chapter 6), in practice guides (covered in Part IV of this chapter), and in CLE materials (discussed in Part VII of this chapter).

A "formbook" may provide actual forms or suggested language that can be used in crafting your document. Examples of California formbooks include *California Forms of Pleading and Practice* (LexisNexis/Matthew Bender) and *California Civil Practice Guide: Civil Procedure Before Trial Forms* (The Rutter Group/Thomson West). Search the library catalog by subject for topical formbooks.

In using any form, take care to ensure that it complies with current law and accurately reflects your client's situation. Forms are designed for general audiences, not a particular client. Before using a form, be sure that you understand every word in the form and that you have modified it, as appropriate, to suit your client's needs. You might also revise the wording to avoid unnec-

---

12. Lexis, Westlaw, and Bloomberg Law also provide access to some documents filed in court, and they provide a searchable database of many court *dockets*. A *docket* is a court's official record of all documents filed in a case. Bloomberg Law currently has the most extensive docket database, including all federal court dockets since 1989 and many California state court dockets. It may be helpful to use these resources to locate court filings that are similar to what you are researching. But use caution in relying on a document filed by another attorney; just because an attorney filed a document in court does not mean that it is correct as to either form or substance.

Table 10-3. Restatement Topics

Agency	Property (Wills and Other Donative Transfers)
Conflict of Laws	
Contracts	Restitution and Unjust Enrichment
Employment Law	Security
Foreign Relations Law of the United States	Suretyship and Guaranty
	Torts
International Commercial Arbitration	Torts: Apportionment of Liability
	Torts: Liability for Economic Harm
Judgments	
Law Governing Lawyers	Torts: Liability for Physical and Emotional Harm
Property	
Property (Landlord & Tenant)	Torts: Products Liability
Property (Mortgages)	Trusts
Property (Servitudes)	Unfair Competition

essary legalese. Do not simply fill in the blanks unless a particular form is prescribed by statute or by a court.

IX. Restatements and Principles of the Law

A restatement is a detailed summary of the common law in a specific legal area. While the *Restatement of Contracts* and the *Restatement of Torts* are the titles familiar to general practitioners, other titles cover a broad range of topics. See Table 10-3.

Restatements result from collaborative efforts by committees of scholars, practitioners, and judges organized by the American Law Institute (ALI). These committees, led by a scholar called the *reporter*, draft text that explains the common law in rule format (i.e., they are written with outline headings similar to statutes, rather than in the narrative form of cases). The committees circulate the drafts for review and revision. The restatement that is published by ALI includes not only the text of the rules that embody the common law but also commentary, illustrations, and notes from the reporter.

Remember that, even though restatements may visually resemble statutes, and lawyers consider restatements influential, restatements are secondary authority. A portion of a restatement may have the force and effect of primary authority for a jurisdiction only if it is adopted by a court in a particular case. For example, in 2016, the California Supreme Court formally adopted a products liability doctrine from the *Restatement of Torts* (3d and 2d), clarifying what circumstances permit a supplier to discharge its duty to warn customers.[13] After a court has adopted a portion of a restatement, the commentary, illustrations, and notes that accompany that particular restatement provision may be valuable tools in understanding the law in that jurisdiction. Cases in other jurisdictions that have adopted the same portion of that restatement would be additional persuasive authority.

Lexis and Westlaw provide access to restatements. To find a relevant restatement in print, search the library catalog for the subject matter or search for *restatement*. When working with print volumes, use the table of contents, index, or appendix to find pertinent sections of a restatement. The text of each restatement section is followed by commentary and sometimes illustrations of key points made in the text. Appendix volumes list citations to cases that have referred to the restatement.

A restatement's language is updated only when a later version is published. However, the appendix volumes are updated with pocket parts and supplements, and online restatement databases are kept current. Shepardizing or KeyCiting a restatement section will reveal cases and articles that cite the restatement.

In addition to restatements, ALI also publishes Principles of the Law in emerging areas of law or areas thought to be in need of reform. For example, one of ALI's current projects is the Principles of the Law in the area of Election Administration, which includes the rules and procedures for recounts and other election disputes. All Principles of the Law, including most drafts, are available online on Westlaw and Lexis.

X. Uniform Laws and Model Codes

The goal of uniform laws and model codes is to harmonize the statutory laws of the fifty states. One of the leading organization in this effort is the National Conference of Commissioners on Uniform State Laws (NCCUSL), which invites law professors, judges, legislators, and attorneys to draft its uniform laws and model codes.

---

13. *Webb v. Electric Co.*, 63 Cal. 4th 167, 187 (2016).

Familiar examples of these secondary sources include the *Uniform Commercial Code* (UCC) and the *Model Penal Code* (MPC). Committees draft proposed language and solicit comments. Then committees finalize the proposed law or code, along with explanatory notes. The published uniform law or model code includes both the proposed statutory language and explanatory notes from the authors.

Generally, research into a uniform law or model code is relevant in California only after the California Legislature enacts it and the governor signs the legislation. Once the proposed language becomes an enacted statute, it is primary authority in California, and the explanatory notes from that uniform law or model code provision become very persuasive secondary authority. For example, every state has adopted a version of the UCC. In researching California's commercial code, you could gain insights from commentary on the UCC that discussed the provisions adopted by California. Additionally, the cases of other states that also adopted the same UCC provisions would be highly persuasive in interpreting California's statute.

Uniform laws and model codes, along with official notes and explanations, are published by their organizational authors. Commercial versions also add commentary and often footnotes with case support. West publishes *Uniform Laws Annotated*, which offers indexing, text, and research annotations to uniform laws prepared under the direction of NCCUSL.

Finding a relevant uniform law or model code is similar to finding a restatement, and many are available on Lexis and Westlaw. In print, search the library catalog for the area of law, such as *commercial transactions* or *criminal law*; you may want to include in your search the words *uniform law* or *model code*. In the stacks, scan the titles nearby to determine whether more helpful commercial editions have been published. Within the volume or set of volumes containing the uniform law or model code, look in the table of contents, index, and appendix to locate relevant sections.

XI. Jury Instructions

California jury instructions are often an effective starting point for research in an unfamiliar area of the law. In addition to outlining the law, each instruction is followed by annotations identifying the cases and statutes that support the instruction. The annotations also cite to relevant treatises and practice guides. See Figure 10-4 for an example of a California Civil Jury Instruction (abbreviated as CACI, which is pronounced "Casey"). Again, this example builds on the client situation in Chapter 1.

Figure 10-4. Example Jury Instruction

California Civil Jury Instructions (CACI)

1621. Negligent Infliction of Emotional Distress—Bystander —Essential Factual Elements

[Name of plaintiff] claims that [he/she] suffered serious emotional distress as a result of perceiving [an injury to/the death of] [name of injury victim]. To establish this claim, [name of plaintiff] must prove all of the following:

1. That [name of defendant] negligently caused [injury to/the death of] [name of injury victim];

2. That [name of plaintiff] was present at the scene of the injury when it occurred and was aware that [name of injury victim] was being injured;

3. That [name of plaintiff] suffered serious emotional distress; and

4. That [name of defendant]'s conduct was a substantial factor in causing [name of plaintiff]'s serious emotional distress.

Emotional distress includes suffering, anguish, fright, horror, nervousness, grief, anxiety, worry, shock, humiliation, and shame. Serious emotional distress exists if an ordinary, reasonable person would be unable to cope with it.

New September 2003

Directions for Use

This instruction is for use in bystander cases, where a plaintiff seeks recovery for damages suffered as a percipient witness of injury to others. If the plaintiff is a direct victim of tortious conduct, use CACI No. 1620, *Negligent Infliction of Emotional Distress—Direct Victim—Essential Factual Elements*.

This instruction should be read in conjunction with either CACI No. 401, *Basic Standard of Care*, or CACI No. 418, *Presumption of Negligence per se*.

In element 2, the phrase "was being injured" is intended to reflect contemporaneous awareness of injury.

Whether the plaintiff had a sufficiently close relationship with the victim should be determined as an issue of law because it is integral to the determination of whether a duty was owed to the plaintiff.

Sources and Authority

- A bystander who witnesses the negligent infliction of death or injury of another may recover for resulting emotional trauma even though he or she did not fear imminent physical harm. (*Dillon v. Legg* (1968) 68 Cal.2d 728, 746—747 [69 Cal.Rptr. 72, 441 P.2d 912].)

Source: Justia website, at www.justia.com/trials-litigation/docs/caci/1600/1621/.

California civil and criminal jury instructions are available on the California courts' website at courts.ca.gov; click on "Courts," then "Jury Service," and then click on "Resources for Court Staff, Judges and Attorneys." Jury instructions are also available in print form from *California Forms of Jury Instruction* (LexisNexis/Matthew Bender), and they are available on Lexis and Westlaw. Note that Westlaw continues to publish the predecessor instructions, *Book of Approved Jury Instructions* or BAJI, even though the California courts' website makes clear that those instructions are no longer officially approved.

XII. Library Guides

Library guides are subject-specific research guides compiled by law librarians who are subject matter experts. A quick Google search for "library guides" reveals that they are now available on most law school library websites. Library guides can be a very helpful place to begin research, especially in an unfamiliar area of the law. Depending on the subject, a library guide may contain suggested resources or even helpful research techniques specific to that area of law.[14]

XIII. Using Secondary Sources in Research

As the discussion above suggests, use of the various secondary sources should be tailored to the needs of individual research projects. For a broad overview of an area of law, Witkin or an encyclopedia may be best. For in-depth analysis of a narrow scholarly topic, a law review article is more likely to be helpful. In litigation, court-approved forms and jury instructions will be indispensable.

Consider your own background in the subject matter and the goals of your research, and select from these sources accordingly. How many secondary sources you use depends on the success of your early searches and the time available to you. Often checking one or two secondary sources is sufficient; you would almost never check every source discussed in this chapter for a single project.

Despite the value of secondary sources, they are rarely cited in memoranda or briefs. Identifying those few secondary sources that may occasionally be appropriate to cite to a senior attorney or a court is a skill you will develop over time. In general, many secondary sources like encyclopedias, A.L.R., and MCLE materials are primarily authority-finding tools and should never be cited. In contrast, Witkin, law review articles, and treatises may be cited on occasion.

Secondary authorities are typically cited when there is no primary authority on point. For example, sometimes writers need to summarize the development of the law. If no case has provided a summary, citing a treatise or law review article which traces that development could be helpful to the reader. Similarly, citation to secondary authority is appropriate when there is no law on point

---

14. The Library of Congress also has what it refers to as "Legal Research Guides," which can be helpful in researching areas of federal law such as federal legislative history.

to support an argument. When arguing to expand or change the law, your only support may come from a law review article or other secondary authority. Finally, secondary authority may provide additional support for a point already supported by primary authority that is only persuasive. For example, you can bolster an argument supported by a case from another jurisdiction by also citing an article or treatise by a respected expert on the topic. Of course, by citing secondary authorities, you are admitting to your audience that you could not locate any primary authority to support your arguments, which may weaken the effectiveness of those arguments.

Regardless of whether you cite a secondary source in a document, you must consider the weight to accord the source in developing your own analysis. The following criteria can be helpful in making that assessment:

- *Author:* A respected judge or professor is more authoritative than a student author or an anonymous editor.
- *Date:* Ensure that the material analyzes the current law. For new legal issues, a recent article is likely to be more helpful than one written decades ago.
- *Publisher:* Material from respected publishers like The Rutter Group will carry more weight than websites by individuals, law firms, or groups with a particular interest.
- *Depth and Relevance:* Unless you just need an overview, the most useful material will be focused specifically on your legal issue and provide thorough analysis.
- *Citation:* A positive citation by a court will make an article or book more persuasive.

Remember that the goals of reading secondary sources are usually to (1) learn about an area of law and (2) locate related primary authority. These goals can be met by referring to secondary sources in books in the library or by skimming them online. Books can be checked out of the library and online sources can be saved to folders, without the waste of printing out numerous pages of text. Moreover, some lengthy secondary sources—for example, law review articles—may initially seem helpful but after a few pages may concentrate on a narrow point that is not applicable to your situation. When working online, try to avoid printing a document until you are sure that you will need to refer to it repeatedly in your research and analysis.

Chapter 11

Planning a Research Strategy and Organizing Research Results

Every research project needs a defined strategy to ensure thorough and efficient research. This chapter quickly reviews the basic research process presented in Chapter 1 and then discusses how to modify it to design a strategy for particular projects. Next, the chapter moves to methods of organizing research results. An organized approach will keep you from getting lost in a morass of papers or online documents and will aid in your analysis of the legal issue.

I. Planning a Research Strategy

The research process presented in Chapter 1 contains six steps:

(1) prepare to research;
(2) learn about the issue by consulting secondary sources;
(3) search for primary authority—meaning constitutional provisions, statutes, administrative regulations, and cases;
(4) read relevant authorities carefully;
(5) update your research by using citators; and
(6) end research when all analytical points have support and when searches in different sources produce the same set of authorities.

The key to successful research is not to follow this process in lockstep, but to mold it to fit each project. On the other hand, you should not wander randomly through these steps; you might forget a step—and miss an important line of authorities—or you might waste valuable time. Instead, begin each project with a defined strategy that considers the legal clues you have as you begin, the sources available, and the goal of the project. These considerations are addressed below.

A. Asking Fundamental Questions

The first step in any research project is to prepare, which requires gathering the relevant facts, identifying the precise issue or issues you need to research, determining the relevant jurisdiction, and listing research terms. Be wary of skipping the step in which you develop research terms, or of trying to do it quickly in your head. If you know the cause of action—and the various ways that indexes or courts may refer to it—that quick approach may work. But some projects get off to a slow start because the researcher did not begin with a thorough list of research terms. If you do not find pertinent material in your early searches, you may need to go back to the beginning and develop a better list of terms.

When you develop your research strategy (essentially, a modified version of the general, six-step process) depends on the project. You might develop a research strategy before you undertake the initial preparatory steps in the previous paragraph, or you might need to do a bit of research first to know what strategy might be effective. In developing your research strategy, ask the following questions:

- Is this issue controlled by state law, federal law, or both?
- Are there statutes or constitutional provisions on point, or is this area controlled by common law?
- Are administrative rules or decisions likely to be involved?
- Where in the research process might print sources be more efficient and cost-effective than online sources?
- What period of time needs to be researched?
- How long do I have to complete the project?

Answering these questions and writing out a strategy will likely make a new project feel less overwhelming because you will see discrete steps that you need to take.

B. Modifying the Process to Create a Focused Strategy

Chapter 1 pointed out a few simple ways that the research process can be modified to suit your research project. To expand on one of those ways, assume that you receive a demand letter from an opponent that cites a case that is directly on point—a significant clue in your research. You should modify the basic research process to reflect what you know. You might write out a research strategy that looks like the following simple checklist:

- read the case
- read any statutes and cases it cites
- search using key numbers on Westlaw
- use KeyCite to update and to find more cases
- check for additional statutes (generate terms first)
- if statutes are on point, check for administrative law
- if any analytical holes are left, consider secondary sources

Your first step in this project should be reading the case, not generating research terms. Next, you may decide to read some of the important cases cited by that case. To find additional cases, you could use key numbers from relevant headnotes in the case to search in Westlaw with West's online digest. Then, running a KeyCite search could find even more cases and would determine whether the case is still respected authority. At some point in reading all of these cases, you may have come across a statute. If so, you should stop and read it, and review its annotations for more cases that may be relevant. You should also consider whether any regulations have addressed the statute. If you have not yet encountered a statute in your search, you should spend a few minutes searching for one. At that point, you would need to generate research terms to search in an annotated code.

If you find strong support for all of your issues, you might never refer to a secondary source in this project. You may, however, decide to do a quick search of a state-specific treatise or practice guide, just to be sure you have not missed anything.

C. Selecting Sources

As you plan your strategy, decide which sources you will use. You should base this decision primarily on which sources are best suited for the task at hand, though you may also consider availability and personal preference. If, for example, your office has a contract with Lexis but not Westlaw, you will naturally choose Shepard's over KeyCite.

1. Researching an Unfamiliar Area of Law

When researching an unfamiliar area of law, you will probably be more successful beginning with secondary sources. Some common research questions and appropriate secondary sources for researching them are discussed next.

a. Typical Practice Issues

Lawyers are faced with fundamental practice tasks every day, such as filing a complaint, conducting depositions, drafting a will or trust, or making a presentation to a client about alternative courses of action. Two very useful tools in these areas are practice guides and state legal encyclopedias. Each is likely to give an overview of the area of law, practice pointers, and even relevant forms and checklists. In California, a Rutter Group practice guide would be an obvious choice among available secondary sources.

b. Cutting-Edge Issues

Often lawyers have to address complex, novel legal issues. Sometimes the answers can be developed or derived from existing primary authorities, with the addition of some common sense and creativity. If there is no primary authority on point — consider the first lawyer faced with the question of whether a police search of a cell phone is the same as a search of a briefcase — a secondary source may be the only authority that has addressed the question in a meaningful way. For instance, the author of a recent law review article may have pondered the same question and produced a thoughtful analysis of the issue. Remember that SSRN, which includes the Legal Scholarship Network, provides access to articles that have not yet been published. They might be the most current source of analysis on a new issue.

c. Surveys

Surveys of the law in multiple jurisdictions can be powerful tools in convincing judges to modify existing law in a particular state. Surveys can also help persuade a court to adopt a new rule favorable to the client when no rule exists in your jurisdiction. A.L.R. annotations usually provide tables that list statutes and cases from every American jurisdiction that has considered a question.

2. Beginning with a Statutory Citation

If you know of a relevant statute, your research project is likely to be most effective if you go directly to an annotated code. It will provide references to cases, to secondary sources discussing the statute, and to the statute's legislative history.

3. Launching from "One Good Case"

Once you find a case that is on point, multiple sources are available for further research. Using Westlaw, you can access Key Numbers by clicking on the words and phrases at the beginning of a headnote (the topic and key number) or you can click the link under the headnotes that gives the number of "Cases that cite this headnote." Another approach is to use the KeyCite links at the top of the screen for the case.

Similarly, on Lexis, clicking on a hyperlinked phrase at the beginning of a headnote will produce a drop-down menu for topic searching (e.g., "View in topic index"). Alternatively, you can highlight text to use in a search. Finally, you can click on "*Shepardize*—Narrow by this Headnote" to jump into the Shepard's results for that case, restricted by that headnote.

D. Sample Research Strategy

To put the discussion above in context, assume that you have been given as a new research task the problem posed in Chapter 1. Your client has suffered nightmares and anxiety attacks after the following scene at a restaurant in San Diego. He and his wife were having lunch at an outside table near the street in the Gaslamp Quarter. The man went inside to use the restroom, and as he was returning to the table he heard a car crash. He saw a table umbrella fall and felt pieces of glass from a shattered mirror. A car had jumped the curb and hit his wife. Although she eventually recovered from her serious injuries, he has continued to suffer symptoms of ongoing distress. He wants to know whether he has a claim against the driver. Assume that you have not researched this issue before and do not know which cause of action might apply. A sample strategy using Lexis products is listed in Table 11-1. Of course, you could conduct a very similar search with primarily West products, selecting *West's* annotated statutes in Step 3, using a full-text search on Westlaw to find

Table 11-1. Sample Research Strategy

- Generate terms. Don't know cause of action, but the general issue is whether the client can recover from the driver.
- Check Witkin in print; look for jury instructions online.
- Check for statutes in *Deering's* in print. Review annotations. If there are statutes, check for pertinent regulations.
- Skim cases referenced so far. Use Lexis drop-down from relevant headnotes for additional cases on the same topics.
- Shepardize authorities on Lexis.
- Create research chart to check analysis.

cases in Step 4, and updating with KeyCite in Step 5. While other online services may offer fewer search options and smaller databases, you can modify the search to be useful for research with Bloomberg Law, Fastcase, Casemaker, VersusLaw, etc.

II. Organizing Research

Legal research often produces many documents that you must organize and analyze. Staying organized is a means to efficient research and thorough legal analysis. Organizational techniques vary among researchers, but the following discussion explains two methods that will help novices working on their first projects. While the first method focuses on working in print and the second focuses on working online, in most situations you will use a combination. For example, you may hand write a list of sources you checked (e.g., books, various online services) but rely on each online service to keep track of specific searches. Similarly, you may use online folders to organize authorities as you encounter them, while printing out the most important documents.

A. Keeping Notes and Documents in Print

Before beginning research, get a three-ring binder or several folders in which you will keep hard copies of the most important authorities you find in your research. Tab the binder or folders with the following headings: strategy/process and lists of primary authorities; secondary sources; statutes (include regulations and constitutional provisions here); cases; and outline. Consider using color-coded sticky notes to tab each new document you add to the binder or folders so that you can find it easily.

As you begin research, create a research strategy/process trail. (This is similar to the "History" created online by Westlaw and Lexis.) This document will record what you actually do as you work through the project. Start with your research strategy document and turn it into a quick summary of what you do as you work. Each time you move to a new step in your research strategy or work with a new resource, make notes in your process trail that summarize your work. For online research, include the site or service, the specific database or link, and the searches that you entered. List both successful and unsuccessful search terms and searches so that (1) you do not inadvertently repeat these same steps later, and (2) you can revisit a seemingly tangential issue that later seems relevant. If you conduct print research, include the volumes you used, the indexes or tables you reviewed, and the terms you searched for. Note when you update authorities

Table 11-2. Process Trail

- Generate terms: anxiety from watching spouse injured; distress; wife; husband; accident; legal theory is likely under a form of negligence.
- Check Witkin in print. Use Table of Contents:

  Torts, Negligence: General Duty, Negligent Causing of Emotional Distress.

  Sections 1022–1023; found *Dillon, Wong, Wooden, Lawson*.

  Jury instructions: found CACI 1621 on Cal. courts website.
- Check for statutes in *Deering's* in print. No statutes on this topic.
- Skim cases referenced so far: *Dillon, Thing*. Review cases cited for headnote 3 of *Thing* (re: not observing accident).
- Shepardize on Lexis. *Thing* led to *Bird* and *Air Crash*.
- Create a research chart to check analysis (see Table 11-3).

---

that you plan to use in your analysis, either by keeping a list of authorities you have updated or by noting on each document when you updated it.

Table 11-2 develops a very brief process trail for the research strategy in Table 11-1. (Yours should be more thorough.) Note that Table 1-3 in Chapter 1 contains a more comprehensive list of research terms.

Create a list that contains the name and citation for each of the primary authorities that you need to read, or open tabs for results you need to investigate carefully. This method will allow you to maintain your train of thought with one resource while ensuring that you keep track of important authorities to check later. After creating a list that includes a number of sources, check for duplicates before reading the authorities.

When researching several issues or related claims, consider them one at a time. In this instance, you may have several lists of primary authorities, one for each claim you are researching. You may want to create different folders for each claim, particularly if each is complex. Only print and keep in the binder authority you intend to use in your analysis, meaning you will likely refer to it frequently.

B. Keeping Notes and Documents Online

The newest generation of online search tools—including Lexis and Westlaw—allows you to keep track of your research and take notes online. The "History" links save searches. The "Folders" allow you to organize your research by saving specific documents to relevant folders for each project you are working on. These two services also allow you to highlight and annotate documents and to share your work with others. While these tools serve experienced researchers well, new researchers are encouraged to use them in tandem with keeping notes as discussed above. Many researchers work more efficiently flipping through a binder or shuffling through a stack of cases than they do opening and scrolling through online files.

III. Organizing Analysis

In addition to taking notes that summarize the research process, keep notes that summarize your analytical progress. Analytical notes provide a basis for organizing your arguments and writing your document. These notes do not have to be formal or typed; you are likely the only person who will read them. The notes should be written in your own words, not cut and pasted from the authorities you find. (Simply cutting and pasting text is easy because it requires little real thinking.) Deciding what is important enough to include in notes and expressing those ideas in your own words will increase your understanding of the legal issues involved.

As you find sources that are not relevant, or that duplicate information better provided by another source, make a few notes on your list of authorities. If a source is not relevant, strike through it on the list, move it to a separate document, or save it in a separate folder. Do not completely delete references to irrelevant authorities or you may later find yourself accidentally reading them again.

Secondary sources. Write a brief summary, perhaps just a paragraph, for each relevant secondary source you consult. Begin the summary with the title, author, and other citation information for the source. In your own words, summarize the relevant analysis in the source, including references to specific pages. Try to include few sentence explaining how this source relates to your research.

Enacted law. Because the exact words of constitutions, statutes, and regulations are so important, you should print the text of these provisions. Then, to fully understand a complex provision, you should outline it. Highlighting is sufficient only if the text is very short and clear. Be sure to refer to the definition sections of statutes; where important terms are not defined, make a note to look for judicial definitions. Also be sure to read statutes that are cross-referenced in any pertinent statute. Check statutory annotations for cross-references to relevant regulations.

Cases. Take notes on all relevant cases by explaining their key components in your own words. Do not waste time with formal case briefs unless they serve your current project; instead, concentrate your efforts on the aspects of the case that affect your analysis. Be sure you understand the procedural posture and the standard of review applied in each case. Also, be sure that you understand the facts of cases. Drawing a timeline or a chart of the relationships between the parties may be helpful. Concentrate your effort on the court's reasoning; too often, novices take notes that focus on facts or general rules, without paying sufficient attention to how the court applied those rules to the specific situation before it. Include the full citation in your notes, and indicate the pages that important ideas come from (i.e., include the pinpoint pages that you will have to cite in a written document). Summarize your thoughts on the case: How do you anticipate using this case in your analysis? Which element does it address? Does it resolve certain issues for your problem? Does it raise new questions?

Updating. When you first look at a source online, note its Shepard's or KeyCite symbol. If the symbol is negative, stop to determine whether the source is still good law before basing your analysis on it. Later, carefully update each authority you use in developing your argument. Consider using an "Alert" function in the citator to keep you posted on any changes as you work on your project. If you need to expand your list of authorities, use updating not only to validate sources but also as a research tool.

Outlining. Because the most effective research often occurs in conjunction with the careful analysis of your particular project, try to develop an outline of your client's legal problem as soon as you can. An initial outline may be based on issues listed in a secondary source, the requirements of a statute, or the elements of a common law claim. If outlining feels too restrictive, consider using a flow chart, index cards, or an analysis box. An analysis box is simply a chart that organizes authorities by issue or element; a sample is shown in Table 11-3, following a description of the client's problem earlier in the chapter. The outline or chart should enable you to synthesize the law, apply the law to your client's facts, and reach a conclusion on the desired outcome.

Table 11-3. Sample Analysis Chart

<u>Research Question</u>: Can a client recover against the driver of a car when he heard but did not see the accident that injured his wife?

Issue	Authority	Case Summary	Client Facts	Conclusion
1. Were client and victim "closely related"?	*Thing*	plaintiff must be a relative living in the same house or a parent, sibling, child, or grand-parent of the victim	injured party was client's wife	client was closely related to the victim
2. Was client "present" at the scene and "then aware" of the injury?	*Wilks*	plaintiff must be instantly aware of likely severe injury; was in different room of house when vacuum exploded; met this element	client heard car crash as it happened; was in the adjacent restaurant	client was present because he was close to the crash scene where he had just left his wife and he knew about the crash as it was happening
	Air Crash	plaintiff watched house burn knowing family was inside because she'd left min-utes before; met this element	client had left his wife at the table moments before	
	Thing	plaintiff was nearby when car crash occurred but wasn't aware of it at the time; did not meet this element	client heard crash, saw umbrella fall, and felt mirror pieces	

IV. Ending Research

For new researchers, it can be difficult to know how much time to devote to a research project and when to stop researching. Deadlines set by a court or a supervisor may limit the time devoted to a project; when the researcher is billing time to the client, that client's ability or willingness to pay will be important.

In the rare situation without these constraints, you can be confident ending your research in the following instances: First, you might find an authority that answers the client's legal question clearly and definitively. Alternatively, when your research in various sources leads back to the same authorities, you can be confident that you have been thorough and stop.

In many situations, though, you will not find a definitive answer but will need to create a solution to the client's problem. If your research does not begin circling back to the same authorities, ending research might feel premature, but you cannot search forever. Review your analytical outline and see whether each point has sufficient support from primary authority in your jurisdiction. If not, look for persuasive authority, either from another jurisdiction or from a respected secondary source. As a final check on your thoroughness, go through each step of the basic research process to ensure you considered each one in your own research strategy for this particular project.

When you are researching a cutting-edge issue, or an issue new to your jurisdiction, you may not find any primary authorities on point. Do not overlook the possibility that nothing exists. Before reaching that conclusion, however, expand your research terms and look in a few more secondary sources. Consider whether other jurisdictions may have helpful persuasive authority. If you have encountered a new legal issue, then you will get to help formulate the law as you assist your client.

Chapter 12

Legal Citation

Lawyers use legal citations to prove that analysis in legal documents is well researched and supported. Legal citations tell the reader where to find the authorities relied on and indicate the level of analytical support the authorities provide.[1] Because citation information is given in abbreviated form, using a uniform and widely recognized format ensures that the reader will understand the information being conveyed.

This chapter explains the format used to convey citation information. The *California Style Manual (CSM)*[2] is explained first. This is the citation manual used by California state courts. Then the chapter turns to the two national citation manuals, the *ALWD Guide to Legal Citation*[3] and *The Bluebook: A Uniform System of Citation*.[4] A lawyer writing to a state court in California has the option of using either the *CSM* or the *Bluebook*, but a single style of citation must be used throughout the document.[5] Note that the *ALWD Guide* produces exactly the same citation format as the *Bluebook* in virtually all instances.

---

1. In practice documents like office memoranda and court briefs, legal citations are typically included in the text of legal documents rather than being placed in footnotes or listed in a bibliography.

2. Edward W. Jessen, *California Style Manual* (4th ed., West 2000) ("*CSM*") (sometimes referred to as the "gold book" or the "orange book"). In this chapter, footnote references to the *CSM* will be to rule numbers (e.g., *CSM* § 1:2[A]).

3. ALWD & Coleen Barger, *ALWD Guide to Legal Citation* (6th ed. 2017) ("*ALWD Guide*"). In this chapter, footnote references to the *ALWD Guide* provide the rule number in this format: *ALWD* Rule 12.2(a).

4. *The Bluebook: A Uniform System of Citation* (The Columbia Law Review et al. eds., 20th ed. 2015) ("*Bluebook*"). In this chapter, footnote references to the *Bluebook* include the rule number in this format: *Bluebook* Rule 18.1. Note that *Bluebook* rules beginning with the letter B apply solely to citations used by practitioners and law clerks; these rules are segregated into *Bluepages* that appear before the rules used for law review footnotes.

5. Cal. R. Ct. Rule 1.200.

Table 12-1. Example Citations from the *California Style Manual*

State Constitution	Cal. Const., art. VI, § 10.
State Statute	Code Civ. Pro. § 340.5.
State Case	*People v. Davis* (1998) 18 Cal.4th 712.
State Rule	Cal. Code Regs., tit. 14, § 916.2.
Law Review Article	Lessig, *The Zones of Cyberspace* (1996) 48 Stan. L.Rev. 1403.

I. The *California Style Manual*

A. Orientation to the *CSM*

The first three chapters of the *California Style Manual* cover citations for cases; constitutions, statutes, and rules; and secondary sources. The fourth chapter addresses matters of style (capitalization, quotations, numbers, italics, and punctuation). The final two chapters explain the editorial policies of the official reporters for California cases and case titles.

The *CSM* has both a table of contents and an index. Both are helpful for finding relevant rules. In addition, each of the six chapters contains a more detailed table of contents. A "Table of Frequently Used Abbreviations" appears at the front of the book, but most of the information is repeated in relevant rules. Those rule-specific lists are often more helpful because similar material can be reviewed quickly. Thus, looking at the list of state and reporter abbreviations in § 1:30 will be easier than looking for each state and reporter in the table in the front of the book.

Following the rules in the *CSM* results in citations that look a bit different from the citations used in other states or in the national citation manuals. Among the most obvious differences are (1) placement of the entire citation in parentheses, (2) the location of the date immediately after the case name, and (3) the use of *supra* in short citations. Even with these cosmetic differences, citations under the *CSM*, the *Bluebook*, and the *ALWD Guide* convey the same essential information. Indeed, the *CSM* relies on the *Bluebook* to fill in any gaps.[6] Examples of *CSM* citations are given in Table 12-1. Brief explanations for case and statutory citations follow.

---

6. *See, e.g., CSM* §§ 1:35, 1:36.

B. Case Citations under the *CSM*

1. Full Citations to Cases

A full citation to a case includes (1) the name of the case, (2) the date the case was decided, (3) the court that decided the case, (4) the volume and abbreviation of the official reporter in which the case was published, (5) the first page of the case, (6) the exact page in the case that contains the idea being cited,[7] and (7) parallel citations, if there are any.[8] Remember that, despite the online availability of cases, citations still reference the print volumes.

EXAMPLES: (*Brown v. Bd. of Educ.* (1955) 349 U.S. 294, 300 [75 S.Ct. 753, 99 L.Ed.1083].)

(*People v. Davis* (1998) 18 Cal.4th 712, 718 [76 Cal.Rptr.2d 770, 958 P.2d 1083].)

(*Flint v. Dennison* (9th Cir. 2007) 488 F.3d 816, 820.)

Use the shortened name of the case from the running head of a print reporter or the shortened name shown in an online source.[9] Words that appear in the table of abbreviations at the front of the *CSM* may be abbreviated; other abbreviations are left to the writer's discretion. See Table 12-5 later in this chapter for selected *CSM* abbreviations, compared to abbreviations used in the national manuals. Between the parties' names, place a lower case "v" followed by a period. Italicize the parties' names and the "v."[10]

Next, in a parenthetical, give the court that decided the case and the jurisdiction, unless both will be clear from the reporter abbreviation.[11] For instance, only decisions of the California Supreme Court are reported in *California Reports,* so citations to that reporter can omit the court and jurisdiction in the parenthetical. Then, in the same parenthetical, give the year the decision was filed.[12]

Following the parenthetical, provide the volume and abbreviation to the relevant print reporter.[13] Abbreviations for California, regional, and federal

---

7. This page is commonly called the *pinpoint* cite, *pincite,* or *jump* cite, though the *CSM* uses the term *point* cite. *CSM* § 1:1[E].

8. *CSM* § 1:1.

9. *CSM* § 1:1[A].

10. *CSM* § 1:1[B].

11. *CSM* § 1:1[D].

12. *Id.*

13. *CSM* § 1:1[E].

Table 12-2. *CSM* Reporter Abbreviations for California Appellate Cases

Reporter	California Decisions Reported	Abbreviations
California Reports	Supreme Court	Cal., Cal.2d, Cal.3d, Cal.4th, Cal.5th
California Appellate Reports	Court of Appeal	Cal.App., Cal.App.2d, Cal.App.3d, Cal.App.4th, Cal.App.5th
West's California Reporter	Supreme Court Court of Appeal from 1959	Cal.Rptr., Cal.Rptr.2d, Cal.Rptr.3d
Pacific Reporter	Supreme Court Court of Appeal through 1959	P., P.2d, P.3d

reporters are included in the table of abbreviations. In addition, abbreviations for California reporters are listed in §§ 1:13 through 1:16, abbreviations for regional reporters are listed in § 1:30, and abbreviations for federal reporters are listed in §§ 1:32[A], 1:33[A], and 1:34[A]. Pay special attention to the series of the reporter, as many reporters are beyond a first series. Note that no spaces appear between abbreviations of reporter titles (i.e., there is no space between Cal. and 4th). In the *Davis* example earlier, 18 is the volume number and Cal.4th is the reporter abbreviation for *California Reports, Fourth Series*. The reporters used for California appellate case citations are summarized in Table 12-2.

After the reporter abbreviation, include both the first page of the case and the page containing the idea that you are referencing, separated by a comma and a space.[14] The first page of the *Davis* case in the earlier example is 712, and the page containing the specific idea being cited is 718.[15]

---

14. *Id.*

15. When using an online version of a case, remember that a reference to a specific reporter page may change in the middle of a computer screen or a printed page. Thus, the page number indicated at the top of the screen or printed page may not be the page where the relevant information is located. For example, if the notation *719 appeared in the text before the relevant information, the pinpoint cite would be to page 719, not page 718.

In brackets following this required information, you may provide parallel citations.[16] You can also note significant subsequent history.[17]

The citation information just explained, based on the location of a case in a print reporter, is preferred. If the case is too recent to have been published in a print reporter, or if the case will only be available online, cite it using the name of parties, court, full date on which the opinion was filed, the court's docket number,[18] and the online citation in brackets. For example, until the following case was available in *California Reports*, it could have been cited as available on Westlaw: (*McClain v. Sav-On Drugs*, (Mar. 4, 2019, S241471) ___ Cal. 5th ___ [2019 WL 1008048].) Other online citation sources include Lexis, the California Daily Opinion Service (abbreviated C.D.O.S.), and the URL on the particular court's website. The bracketed citation to Westlaw or other online sources is helpful, but not required.

2. Short Citations to Cases

After a full citation has been used once to introduce an authority, short citations are subsequently used to cite to the same authority. If a case will be cited frequently, a shortened version of the case name can be used after the full citation. This shortened version may be simply the name of the first party listed.[19]

Within the same paragraph, use *ibid.* to cite the identical page in the case. Use *id.* followed by "at p." and the page number to refer to a different page of the same case. Note that *ibid.* and *id.* can be used only to refer to a case already cited in the same paragraph and only if no other citations have intervened.

> EXAMPLE: In *People v. Davis* (1998) 18 Cal.4th 712, 714, the defendant argued for reversal of a burglary conviction. The defendant had placed a forged check in a chute at a check-cashing business's walk-up facility. (*Ibid.*) After an extensive review of the crime of burglary in California, the Supreme Court agreed that no burglary had taken place. (*Id.* at p. 724.)

To cite a case in a later paragraph (or in the same paragraph after an intervening citation), use the case name, *supra*, the reporter volume and abbreviation, and the relevant pinpoint page numbers.

> EXAMPLE: (*Davis, supra*, 18 Cal.4th at p. 715.)

---

16. *CSM* § 1:1[F]. Including parallel citations is better practice. *CSM* § 1:12.
17. *CSM* § 1:11.
18. Docket numbers are explained in *CSM* § 1:17[B].
19. *CSM* § 1:1[C].

Table 12-3. Introductory Signals

No signal	• The source cited provides direct support for the idea in the sentence.
	• The citation identifies the source of a quotation.
See	• The source cited offers indirect support for the idea in the sentence.
	• The source cited offers support in dicta.
	• The source cited offers support in a concurring or dissenting opinion.
See also	• The source cited provides additional support for the idea in the sentence.
	• The support offered by *see also* is indirect.
E.g.	• The source cited is representative of other authorities that support the idea explained in the sentence.

3. Signals

A citation also conveys the level of support each authority provides by including or omitting introductory signals. The strongest support is shown by using no signal. The more common signals are explained in Table 12-3.[20]

4. Explanatory Parentheticals

After a citation, a short parenthetical can help show the relationship between the cited authority and the idea in the text.[21] The most effective parentheticals are very brief descriptions of the facts or holding of the case or short quotes. Complete sentences are disfavored in parentheticals.

EXAMPLE: The California Supreme Court has stated in dicta that inserting a hand into a library chute to steal books would constitute burglary. (*See People v. Davis* (1998) 18 Cal.4th 712, 723 [holding that passing a forged check through a chute at a check-cashing business was not burglary]).

20. *CSM* § 1:4.
21. *CSM* § 1:6.

C. Statutory Citations under the *CSM*

A citation to a California statute requires both the abbreviated name of the code[22] and the section number.[23] Code abbreviations are listed in § 2:8. To show a subdivision of a particular statutory section, use the abbreviation "subd."

A citation to a federal statute includes the title number, code abbreviation, and section number. Subdivisions are shown by enclosing the letter in parentheses. While citation to the official *United States Code* (U.S.C.) is preferred, citation to either *United States Code Annotated* (U.S.C.A.) or *United States Code Service* (U.S.C.S.) is acceptable under the *CSM*. Note that federal statutes do not have code names like California statutes have. Note also that a statutory citation includes neither a publisher nor a date.

> EXAMPLES: (Code Civ. Proc., § 564, subd. (a).)
>   (28 U.S.C. § 1441(a).)

D. Quotations

The *CSM* provides clear instruction on quotations: "Quoted material should correspond exactly with its original source in wording, spelling, capitalization, internal punctuation, and citation style."[24] All modifications, additions, or deletions must be shown. The rules for quoted material are provided in *CSM* § 4:12 through § 4:27.

II. National Citation Manuals

The two most widely used national citation manuals are the *ALWD Guide* and the *Bluebook*. Both are large booklets that contain hundreds of pages of citation rules, examples, and explanations. The *ALWD Guide* is considered by many the best citation manual for novices and for practitioners. The explanations are clear, and most of the examples are given in the format required in the memoranda and briefs attorneys write. The *Bluebook* is the oldest, most widely known citation manual. Most of the *Bluebook*'s explanations and examples are formatted for law review footnotes, which use different fonts (e.g., large and small capitals) than those used in citations for practice documents.

---

22. *CSM* § 2:8.
23. *CSM* § 2:5[A], 2:6.
24. *CSM* § 4:27.

Under the current editions (6th for the *ALWD Guide* and 20th for the *Bluebook*), citations for practitioner documents are intended to be identical. Even so, attorneys often use the term "Bluebooking" to mean checking citations for accuracy and consistent format.

A. Navigating the *ALWD Guide* and the *Bluebook*

1. Index

The index at the back of each manual is quite extensive, and in most instances, it is more helpful than the table of contents. Most often, you should begin working with a citation manual by referring to the index.

2. "Fast Formats" and "Quick Reference"

Many chapters of the *ALWD Guide* begin with citation examples, in tables called "Fast Formats." A list of these "Fast Formats" is provided on the inside front cover of the *ALWD Guide*.

The *Bluebook* contains two "Quick Reference" guides. The one on the inside front cover provides sample citations for law review footnotes. The guide on the inside back cover gives example citations for court documents (e.g., briefs) and legal memoranda. Be sure to consult the appropriate guide for your writing task because the citations may differ depending on the document you are drafting.

3. Alternate Formats: *ALWD* "FN" Rules and *Bluebook* "Bluepages"

Both the *ALWD Guide* and the *Bluebook* provide instructions for citation in documents for law practice and for citation in the footnotes of academic articles and books. The two manuals take different approaches in displaying the different citation formats.

Most of the citations in the *ALWD Guide* are in practitioner format. Where the format for academic articles and books would be different, the *ALWD Guide* immediately follows the practitioner format with a rule explaining the academic format. These rules are designated with "FN" and accompanied by an "Academic Formatting" icon.

In contrast, the *Bluebook* segregates treatment of practitioner and academic citation rules. The *Bluebook* opens with a short section devoted to citations for practitioners. These "Bluepages" provide information for and examples of citations used in documents other than law review articles.[25] The bulk of the

---

25. The Bluepages are helpful in knowing which font to use in citations in legal memoranda and court documents. The Bluepages list the following items that should

Bluebook is devoted to academic citation format. When using the *Bluebook*, remember that only the Bluepages and the quick reference guide at the back of the manual provide examples for practice documents. Thus, a lawyer using the *Bluebook* must use the Bluepages to translate examples in the rest of the manual from law review format into the format used in practice documents.

4. *ALWD* Appendices and *Bluebook* Tables

The back section of each citation manual contains lists of abbreviations and other helpful information. In the *ALWD Guide* these are called "appendices."[26] Pages with dark blue edges at the back of the *Bluebook* contain "tables" with similar information.[27]

B. Citing California Material

Because these manuals are designed for national use, their citations for California material vary from California practice. A summary of abbreviations for California material appears in Appendix 1 of the *ALWD Guide* and in Table T1.3 of the *Bluebook*. Examples for citations in briefs and memoranda are included in Table 12-4 in this chapter. Compare these examples to the California citations shown in Table 12-1.

---

be italicized or underlined in citations in legal memoranda and court documents: case names, titles of books and articles, and introductory signals. Items not included in the list should appear in regular type. Remember to follow the typeface instructions in the Bluepages even when other *Bluebook* examples include large and small capital letters.

26. Especially helpful *ALWD Guide* appendices are Appendix 1 (federal and state sources for primary authority); Appendix 3(A), 3(B)(1), and 3(E) (abbreviations for months, states, and case names, respectively); Appendix 4 (abbreviations for court names); and Appendix 5(A) (abbreviations for periodicals).

27. Especially helpful *Bluebook* tables are Table T1.1 (sources for federal cases and legislative materials); Table T1.2 (sources for federal administrative and executive materials); Table T1.3 (state sources, listed alphabetically by state); Table T6 (case name abbreviations); Table T12 (month abbreviations); and Table T13 (periodical abbreviations).

**Table 12-4. Example California Citations in *ALWD* and
Bluebook Practitioner Format**

Type of Document	Citation
State Constitution	Cal. Const., art. VI, § 10.
State Statute	Cal. Civ. Proc. Code § 340.5 (West 2006).
State Case	*People v. Davis*, 18 Cal. 4th 712, 714 (1998).
State Regulation	Cal. Code Regs., tit. 14, § 916.2 (2018).
Law Review Article	Lawrence Lessig, *The Zones of Cyberspace*, 48 Stan. L. Rev. 1403 (1996).

C. Case Citations

As with the *CSM*, case citations under *ALWD* and *Bluebook* rules are most often to print reporters.

1. Full Citations to Cases

In both *ALWD* and *Bluebook* format, a full case citation provides the following information about the case:

- the name of the case;
- the volume and reporter in which the case is published;
- the first page of the case;
- the page in the case containing the idea being cited (i.e., the *pinpoint* or *jump* cite);
- the court that decided the case; and
- the year the case was decided.[28]

The key points for citation to cases are given below, along with examples.

Include the name of the first party on each side, even if several are listed in the case caption. For individuals, include only the party's family name. For a business or organization, shorten the party's name by using abbreviations provided in the citation manual.[29] Some common abbreviations appear in Table 12-5 in this section. Note that the *CSM* abbreviates fewer words than either of the national manuals and that "United States" is never abbreviated when it is a party's name.[30]

---

28. *ALWD* Rule 12; *Bluebook* Rule B10 and 10.
29. *ALWD* Appendix 3(E); *Bluebook* Table T6.
30. *ALWD* Rule 12.2(h); *Bluebook* Rule 10.2.2.

Table 12-5. Comparison of Selected Abbreviations in CSM, ALWD, and *Bluebook* Formats

Word	CSM	ALWD (Appendix 3) Bluebook (Table T.6)
Associate	*	Assoc.
Association	Assn.	Ass'n
Center	*	Ctr.
Community	*	Cmty.
Department	Dept.	Dep't
Lawyer	Law.	*
National	Nat.	Nat'l
Partnership	*	P'ship
Resource[s]	*	*
University	U. or Univ.	Univ.

* No abbreviation provided.

Most cases have a lower case "v" followed by a period between the parties' names. (Cases about property, for example, may begin with *In re* and not include a v.[31]) The parties' names and the "v" may be italicized or underlined, but use one style consistently in each citation and throughout each document.[32] Note that using italics avoids confusing readers on an electronic platform who may see underlining as a hyperlink. Put a comma after the second party's name, but do not italicize or underline this comma.

EXAMPLES: *Flint v. Dennison*, 488 F.3d 816, 820 (9th Cir. 2007).

Flint v. Dennison, 488 F.3d 816, 820 (9th Cir. 2007).

Next, give the volume number and the reporter abbreviation, noting carefully the reporter series (e.g., first, second, third, fourth).[33] In the *Flint* example,

---

31. *ALWD* Rule 12.2(p) and *Bluebook* Rule 10.2.1.

32. *ALWD* Rule 12.2(a)(1) (case names) and Rule 1.1 (typeface choice); *Bluebook* Rule B2.

33. Abbreviations for common reporters are found in Chart 12.2 of the *ALWD Guide*; abbreviations for reporters for California cases are included in Appendix 1. The *Bluebook* does not have a comprehensive list of common reporters; check Table T1.1 for federal reporters and Table 1.3 for state reporters by jurisdiction. For cases available only on Lexis or Westlaw, follow *ALWD* Rule 12.14(b) and *Bluebook* Rules B10.1.4 and 18.3.

488 is the volume number and F.3d is the abbreviation for *Federal Reporter*'s third series.

Following the reporter abbreviation, include the first page of the case and the pinpoint page (or pages) containing the idea that you are referencing. Separate the first and pinpoint pages by a comma and a space.[34] In the *Flint* example, 816 is the first page of the case, and 820 is the page containing the idea being cited. If the idea being cited appears on two consecutive pages, show that by repeating the last two digits after a hyphen or en-dash (e.g., 820–21).[35] In the rare instances when the pinpoint page is also the first page, the same page number will appear twice (e.g., 816, 816).

After this information about how to find the case, indicate the court that decided it and that court's jurisdiction.[36] This indication will often be abbreviations in a parenthetical. In Appendix 1 of the *ALWD Guide* and in Table T1 of the *Bluebook*, the abbreviations for the courts of each jurisdiction are included in parentheses just after the name of the court. In the *Flint* example, the federal Ninth Circuit Court of Appeals decided the case; that court is abbreviated 9th Cir. (do not use superscript for ordinals like 9th).

When the reporter abbreviation already indicates the court that decided a case and its jurisdiction, do not repeat that information in the parenthetical. For example, when citing a California Supreme Court case to the official reporter, *California Reports*, there is no need for any additional information about the court in the parenthetical. The reporter abbreviation "Cal. 4th" shows that the jurisdiction is California, and the highest court is presumed unless otherwise noted. To cite the same case to the *Pacific Reporter, Third Series*, abbreviated "P.3d," the deciding court needs to be indicated parenthetically. In the second example below, "Cal." indicates that the decision came from the California Supreme Court rather than from another court whose decisions are also published in the *Pacific Reporter*.

EXAMPLES: *Brown v. Bd. of Educ.*, 349 U.S. 294, 300 (1955).

Ketchum v. Moses, 17 P.3d 735, 736 (Cal. 2001).

West's California Reporter publishes cases from both the California Supreme Court and the California Courts of Appeal. The reporter name makes clear

---

34. *ALWD* Rules 5 and 12.5; *Bluebook* Rule B10.1.2.

35. When reading a case online, remember that a reference to a specific reporter page may change in the middle of a computer screen or a printed page. *See* note 15 *supra*.

36. *ALWD* Rule 12.6(a); *Bluebook* Rule B10.1.3.

that a case is from a California court. If there is no court designation, as in the first case below, the reader assumes the case is from the state Supreme Court. All citations to California Court of Appeal cases in that reporter must include the court designation in the parenthetical, as in *People v. Wise* in the example below. When citing to Court of Appeal cases published in *West's California Reporter*, do not include the particular district unless it is highly relevant.[37]

EXAMPLE: *People v. Buza*, 230 Cal. Rptr. 3d 681 (2018).

People v. Wise, 30 Cal. Rptr. 2d 413 (Ct. App. 1994).

The date the case was decided is provided in the parenthetical containing any abbreviations for the court and jurisdiction. For cases published in reporters, give only the year of decision.[38] For cases available only online, give the month abbreviation, date, and year.[39]

Prior and subsequent history are added to the end of a citation. While important subsequent history is required, prior history is included only if it is particularly relevant to the idea you are referencing, as shown in the example below.[40]

EXAMPLE: The California Supreme Court recently upheld the constitutionality of a law requiring all persons arrested for felony offenses to submit to a cheek swab DNA sample. *People v. Buza*, 4 Cal. 5th 658, 691 (2018), *rev'g* 213 Cal. App. 4th 1446 (2014).

2. Short Citations to Cases

Using full case citations throughout a document would add unnecessary length and could distract readers. Thus, after giving the full citation to introduce an authority, you should use short citation format.[41] When the immediately preceding cite is to the same source and the same page, use *id.* as the short cite. When the second cite is to a different page within the same source, follow the *id.* with "at" and the new pinpoint page number. Capitalize *id.* when it begins a citation sentence, but use lower case otherwise.[42]

---

37. *ALWD* Rule 12.6(c)(4); *Bluebook* Rule 10.4.
38. *ALWD* Rule 12.7; *Bluebook* Rules B10.1.3 and 10.5.
39. *ALWD* Rule 12.7 and 12.14(b); *Bluebook* Rule B10.1.4.
40. *ALWD* Rules 12.8–12.9; *Bluebook* Rule B10.1.6 and 10.7 (listing exceptions when subsequent history may be omitted).
41. *ALWD* Rules 12.16, 11.2, 11.3; *Bluebook* Rule B10.2.
42. *ALWD* Rule 11.3(b); *Bluebook* Rule B10.2.

When you are citing a previously cited case that is not the immediately preceding cite, your short cite needs to provide more information for clarity. In this instance, provide the name of one of the parties (generally the first party named in the full cite), the volume, the reporter, and the pinpoint page following "at."[43] A correct example is "*Davis*, 18 Cal. 4th at 714." The format "*Davis* at 714," consisting of just a case name and page number, is incorrect. Note, too, that mentioning the name of the case in a sentence does not allow you to use *id.* as the citation if the immediately preceding cite is to a different authority. The following example illustrates the use of full and short citations using *ALWD* and *Bluebook* format.

> EXAMPLE: In *People v. Davis*, 18 Cal. 4th 712, 714 (1998), the defendant argued for reversal of a burglary conviction. The defendant had placed a forged check in a chute at a check-cashing business's walk-up facility. *Id.* After an extensive review of the crime of burglary in California, the Supreme Court disapproved *People v. Ravenscroft*, 198 Cal. App. 3d 639 (1988), on which the prosecution had relied, and agreed that no burglary had taken place. *Davis*, 18 Cal. 4th at 724.

D. Federal Statutory Citations

Cite federal laws to the *United States Code* (U.S.C.), the official code for federal statutes, when that series contains the current statutory language.[44] Given the multi-year lag time in publication of U.S.C., the current language will likely be found in a commercial version, either *United States Code Annotated* (U.S.C.A., published by West) or *United States Code Service* (U.S.C.S., published by LexisNexis).

The citation to a federal statute includes the following:

- the title number;
- the code abbreviation;
- the section number;
- the publisher (except for U.S.C., which is published by the government); and
- the date of the volume in which the statute is published (not the date the statute was enacted).

Determining the appropriate date to include can be particularly challenging if the statute has been amended since the bound volume was published. If the

---

43. *ALWD* Rule 12.16; *Bluebook* Rule B10.2.
44. *ALWD* Rule 14; *Bluebook* Rule B12.1.1.

language appears only in the pocket part or supplement, include only the date of the pocket part or supplement.[45] If the language of only a portion of the statute is reprinted in the pocket part or supplement, include the dates of both the bound volume and the pocket part or supplement.[46]

EXAMPLE: 43 U.S.C.A. § 1786 (West Supp. 2018).
            (Statutory language appears in the pocket part only)

EXAMPLE: 43 U.S.C.A. § 1543 (West 2007 & Supp. 2018).
            (Statutory language appears in both the bound volume
            and the pocket part)

E. Signals

Introductory signals show the type of support each cited authority provides. Some authorities state an idea explicitly (meaning you would use no signal), while other authorities might support a proposition only by inference (meaning you would use the signal *see*). Table 12-3, which appears earlier in the chapter, explains the more frequently used signals.[47]

F. Explanatory Parentheticals

Both the *ALWD Guide* and the *Bluebook* provide for explanatory parentheticals following citations, similar to parentheticals under the *CSM*.[48] Parenthetical information can convey various types of information to the reader:

- the weight of the authority (e.g., a case may have been decided *en banc* or *per curiam*);
- brief, but helpful, details about the case (especially useful after the signal *see*);
- the split in decision among the judges who heard the case (e.g., 5–4); and
- the names of judges who joined in a dissenting, concurring, or plurality opinion.[49]

---

45. *ALWD* Rules 8.1 and 14.2(f)(2); *Bluebook* Rules 3.1 and 12.3.2.
46. *ALWD* Rules 8.3 and 14.2(f); *Bluebook* Rules 3.1 and 12.3.2.
47. *ALWD* Rule 35; *Bluebook* Rule B1.2.
48. *ALWD* Rule 37; *Bluebook* Rules B1.3 and B10.1.5.
49. *ALWD* Rule 12.10; *Bluebook* Rule B10.1.5 and 1.5.

EXAMPLE: *Madison Cty. v. Oneida Indian Nation of N.Y.*, 562 U.S. 42 (2011) (per curiam) (vacating and remanding in light of new facts).

Because readers tend to skim citations, and especially parentheticals within citations, be careful not to hide important analysis in a parenthetical at the end of a long citation.

G. Quotations

In every legal citation system, the words, punctuation, and capitalization of a quote must appear exactly as they are in the original.[50] While you must attribute with quotation marks any words that you draw directly from a case, statute, or other source, you should avoid quoting except when those words are particularly significant. Any alterations to or omissions from the quoted text must be indicated. If you need to use too many ellipses or brackets to indicate changes, consider paraphrasing instead of quoting. Include commas and periods inside quotation marks; place other punctuation outside the quotation marks unless it is included in the original text. And try to provide smooth transitions between your text and the quoted text.

H. Numbers and Abbreviations

It is most common in legal documents to spell out numbers zero through ninety-nine and to use numerals for larger numbers. Some legal writers prefer to write out only numbers zero to nine. However, you must always spell out a number that is the first word of a sentence.[51]

Ordinal abbreviations can be confusing. In citations, do not use superscript in creating ordinal abbreviations. In other words, use "9th" not "9th." Note that two ordinal abbreviations, 2d and 3d, are different in legal citations from common non-legal format (2nd and 3rd).[52] Those common forms are still used in text.

Do not insert a space between abbreviations of single capital letters. For example, there is no space in U.S. Moreover, ordinal numbers like 1st, 2d, and 3d are considered single capital letters for purposes of this rule. Thus,

---

50. *ALWD* Rule 38.2 says, "Present quotations accurately; reproduce words exactly as they appear in the original source. Never misrepresent a quotation's original meaning...."). Rules 38, 39, and 40; *Bluebook* Rule B5.

51. *ALWD* Rule 4.2; *Bluebook* Rules B6 and 6.2(a).

52. *ALWD* Rule 4.3; *Bluebook* Rule 6.2(b).

there is no space in P.2d or F.3d because 2d and 3d are considered single capital letters. Leave one space on each side of elements of an abbreviation that are not single capital letters. As examples, Cal. Rptr. 3d has a space between each component, and F. Supp. 3d has a space on each side of "Supp."[53]

III. *ALWD* and *Bluebook* Citations for Law Review Articles

While the rules discussed above also apply to citations in footnotes to law review articles, the *ALWD Guide* and the *Bluebook* use different fonts—including large and small capital letters—for law review citations. Moreover, these citations are placed in footnotes, not embedded within the text of the article.[54] Table 12-6 of this chapter summarizes the typeface used for several common sources and gives examples.

The typeface used for a case name depends on (1) whether the case appears in the main text of the article or in a footnote and (2) how the case is used.[55]

- When a case name appears in the main text of the article or in a textual sentence of a footnote, it is italicized.
- When a footnote contains an embedded citation, the case name is written in ordinary type.
- When a full cite is given in a footnote, the case name is written in ordinary type.
- When a short cite is used in footnotes, the case name is italicized.

IV. Citations Not Covered by a Manual

Although the *CSM*, the *ALWD Guide*, and the *Bluebook* are tediously comprehensive, they do not definitively answer every citation question. When you cannot find a specific rule to cover a source you need to cite, look for rules regarding analogous sources. In any situation when you cite without specific rules dictating the format, be guided by the purpose of citation: to allow a reader to find a source and to understand the type and weight of support it provides.

---

53. *ALWD* Rule 2.2; *Bluebook* Rule 6.1.
54. *ALWD* Rule 34.1; *Bluebook* Rule 1.1.
55. *See ALWD* Rule 12.2(a)(2) and *Bluebook* Rules 10.2 and 10.9.

Table 12-6. Typeface for Law Review Footnotes

Item	Type used	Example
Cases	Use ordinary type for case names in full citations. (See text for further explanation.)	Legal Servs. Corp. v. Velazquez, 531 U.S. 533 (2001).
Statutes	Use large and small capitals for code names.	Cal. Penal Code § 451 (West 2016).
Books	Use large and small capital letters for the author and the title.	Meagan McAlpin, Beyond the First Draft (2014).
Periodical articles	Use ordinary type for the author's name, italics for the title, and large and small capitals for the periodical.	Linda Berger, *Lies Between Mommy and Daddy: The Case for Recognizing Spousal Emotional Distress Claims Based on Domestic Deceit that Interferes with Parent-Child Relationships*, 33 Loy. L.A. L. Rev. 417 (2000).
Explanatory phrases	Use italics for all explanatory phrases, such as *aff'g*, *cert. denied*, *rev'd*, and *overruled by*.	Legal Servs. Corp. v. Velazquez, 531 U.S. 533 (2001), *aff'g* 164 F.3d 757 (2d Cir. 1999).
Introductory signals	Use italics for all introductory signals, such as *see* and *e.g.* when they appear in citations, as opposed to text.	*See id.*

About the Authors

Aimee Dudovitz is a Clinical Professor of Law at Loyola Law School, Los Angeles. After receiving her J.D. from the University of California, Davis, School of Law, she clerked for the Honorable Harry Pregerson of the Ninth Circuit Court of Appeals and for the Honorable Dean D. Pregerson of the Central District of California. She practiced law in Los Angeles for nine years, including with Irell & Manella LLP and Strumwasser & Woocher LLP.

Sarah Laubach is a Professor of Legal Writing at University of California, Berkeley School of Law, where she has taught since 2008. Prior to teaching, she clerked for the Honorable A. Wallace Tashima of the Ninth Circuit Court of Appeals and practiced law at the civil rights firm of Rosen Bien Galvan & Grunfeld in San Francisco.

Suzanne E. Rowe began her legal career clerking for the Honorable Rudi M. Brewster of the Southern District of California. She has taught legal research and writing at the University of San Diego School of Law, Florida State University College of Law, and the University of Oregon School of Law, where she is currently the James L. and Ilene R. Hershner Professor. She is a graduate of Columbia University School of Law.

Index